IN THE NAME OF GOD

Entrepreneurship as done by

Ali Asghar Amiri

The Founder of
Espinas hotels chain

Written by:
Dr. Reza Yadegari
Dr. Mahshid Sanaeefard
The Winners of the Prestigious
Jalal Al-e Ahmad Literary Award
and
Aryaan Yadegari
Lilyaan Yadegari
The Second Generation Authors of the
Great Iranian Entrepreneur Book Collection Set

Serial Number: P 2546190218
Title: Entrepreneurship as done by **Ali Asghar Amiri**
Sub Title: The Founder of Espinas Hotels Chain
Authors: Dr. Reza Yadegari & Dr. Mahshid Sanaeefard
Co-Authors: Aryaan Yadegari &Lilyaan Yadegari
ISBN: 978-1-77892-143-8
Metadata: Biography & Entrepreneurship
Book Size: Paperback
Pages: 120
Canada Publish Date: February 2025
Publisher: Kidsocado Publishing House

Copyright @ 2025 By Kidsocado Publishing House
All Rights Reserved, including the right of production in whole or in part in any form.

Kidsocado Publishing house
Vancouver, Canada

WhatsApp: +1 (236) 333 7248
Email: info@kidsocado.com
https://kidsocado.com

Content

- Introduction 3
- The Greenlight 5
- The life and world of Ali Asghar Amiri 9
- The analysis of the founder of Espinas hotels chain 84

Introduction

The work of identifying the greatest Iranian entrepreneurs got underway back in 1997 with the help and assistance of my wife Dr. Mahshid Sanaeefard, the Manager of the Great Iranian Entrepreneurs Publication. An exceptionally long and arduous task, which has enabled us to gain substantial insight into the world of entrepreneurship and job creation, and thus make history for the future generation of Iranians by helping found and chart a whole new path towards true success in business and industry alike.

Next to winning numerous international awards on this incredible journey of countless ups and downs, we have cooperated and collaborated extensively with some of Iran's highly accredited and most reputable higher learning centers, like Sharif Industrial University, University of Science and Technology, Alzahra University and Shahid Beheshti University. Moreover, we have also successfully established and registered the International Qualification and Certification Auditors Company or IQCA in Canada, whose main role and responsibility is to publish the life history of the greatest Iranian entrepreneurs to make them known by name to the other people in the world. IQCA has also been highly active in setting up and establishing an award presentation scheme in Iran in order to identify and introduce the country's most creative individuals and organizations, and thereby aid and assist with promoting them on a global scale.

It is hoped that as a special and leading group, we are able to introduce the most powerful Iranian women and me to the rest of the world and at the same time, identify and retell the life stories of the best role models for Iran's next generation.

Dr. Reza Yadegari
www.UNESCO.ws
www.09128989113.com

The Greenlight

The movement to transfer the experiences of the world's greatest entrepreneurs is one of the most important factors in helping the American and European companies and organizations' progress and improvement. These companies and organizations had concluded rather smartly that if a society wishes significant advancement and development, it must keep its eye on the experiences of the previous generation and not allow the young to incur costs on the system by experiencing and learning through trial and error. In line with the same notion, entrepreneurship has the potential to create notable transformation throughout a given society's various levels provided it is implemented using principles and plans that take advantage of the experiences of the proficient and skilled members. Allowing the young to take over across the world is certainly a commendable measure, which has also been taken in our beloved Iran as well, except that here the experiences of the previous generation of entrepreneurs and managers has never been made properly available for application by the new generation – something that has regrettably inflicted irrecoverable costs onto the country because of the continuous repetition of the same old mistakes. Our project to identify the greatest Iranian entrepreneurs, so that we may research their lives to understand the reasons and factors for their success started off back in 1997 simultaneously as the arrival of the novel science of entrepreneurship in Iran. Admittedly, the path has been a long one involving strenuous effort. In the years following the events of the Iranian Revolution, literary no entrepreneur in the country was willing to unveil and reveal herself or himself and the experiences she or he possessed.

In spite of this, we were quite determined to fulfil our goal of teaching and training the future generation by documenting and publishing the life stories and experiences of Iran's greatest entrepreneurs through a one-thousand-volume book aptly titled 'Entrepreneurship as done by …' What is presented in the book collection, is rare and valuable roadmap designed based on the experiences and performances of Iran's greatest economic minds, which undoubtedly can be a wonderful asset in guiding and directing anyone who intends to get involved in any type of commercial, production and service provision activity. We hope that our collection book can help open up doors and pave the way for Iran's new generation of young entrepreneurs, and also remain a lasting piece of literary work to remember us by.

Dr. Reza Yadegari
Dr. Mahshid Sanaeefard
Tehran, Iran 2021

Once again, I begin my words with respect before the sacred presence of the Creator, whose boundless blessings are upon me. He has bestowed upon me patient motivations and positive thinking, so that with such a blessing, I may wholeheartedly pursue my goals; also I send heartfelt greetings and salutations to the exalted spirits of my beloved mother and father, from whom I have had the privilege of being born into such a cherished family.

I am from Yazd, a province in the heart of the desert, a land inhabited by hardworking, diligent, tireless, and patriotic people who spare no effort or sacrifice in striving for the pride and elevation of the name of Iran and Iranians and their reasoning often aligns with this saying:

‹Have great ambition, since the great men of the time
Have achieved success through their high aspirations.›

There have always been and will always be discouraging factors and demotivating elements in every time and situation; We must strengthen our wisdom and self-confidence, and with a clear plan and objective, look at the issues around us, and based on that, overcome the obstacles.

I remember that I started working around the age of 12. With hard work, positive thinking, and purposeful planning; I was able to establish a knitting workshop with several workers before I turned 18.

Friends, let›s not allow existing limitations to lead us to despair and frustration on the path we are pursuing.

Let's draw from the proven experiences of successful individuals. Use of thoughtful advisors in specific situations where decision-making becomes difficult and hinders our progress can be very beneficial, since a worthy person will resolve any obstructive barrier and continue his path to the advance.

There is no problem or obstacle that cannot be solved with insight and intelligence; it requires patience and hard work, which, by God›s grace, we are fortunate to possess.

With hope for better and more successful future, and ultimately, under the shade of effort, diligence, and positive thinking, while avoiding laziness and complacency, may we witness a beloved, prosperous and proud Iran in the world. Hoping for that day.

Under the protection of the Almighty God.

Ali Asghar Amiri»

The Life and world of
Ali Asghar Amiri

The desert... Silence... Peace... All I see is beauty, an endless expanse where the eye, no matter how far it wanders, finds no boundary. But why should it? How could one tear away from such grandeur and vastness? It's all hills and valleys, hardships and ease. In this place, one feels closer to God than ever before. It's as if the sky is within your grasp, as if, with just a few more steps, you might meet God, see angels lined up in heaven, glorifying the Creator of all things.

"What's going on? Why did the bus stop?"

My father's voice, coming from beside me, broke the stillness. A murmur spread through the bus. Everyone had something to say:

"Our luck just ran out. Looks like the bus broke down."

"Great! What are we going to do now, in the middle of nowhere?"

Then, the driver's voice cut through the commotion, silencing everyone for a moment:

"Alright, everyone, off the bus. I need to change the tire... It'll take about twenty minutes."

Complaints rose from several passengers, including my mother, who couldn't bear the heat. We all had no choice but to get off the bus. My father, mother, and siblings, like most of the passengers, huddled in the shade of the bus, waiting for the driver to call us back on board. A few men gathered around the driver, helping him change the tire.

Perhaps the only one who found joy in the situation was me. This unexpected stop had given me a moment to commune with the beautiful desert. With every glance across the vastness, I could grasp the secret of life, read a story, and learn a lesson. Watching the shifting sands, which would sometimes form a mound only to flatten out moments later, taught me a profound truth:

Look, human! Gaze upon this beautiful scene… Know that no hardship lasts forever. Just as these mounds of sand rise only to be leveled again, so too do difficulties in life fade away. Conversely, do not assume that life will always be smooth and easy, for the winds of fate may build obstacles in your path. Yet, these obstacles are not permanent; instead, they bring lessons that must be learned before you move forward.

This masterpiece of God, this vast and magnificent painting, offers even more lessons. It teaches us that neither the peak of status nor rank should fill us with arrogance, nor should we lose hope when trapped in the depths of hardship and despair. Life, like the desert, is filled with highs and lows. One moment you're on top of the world, and the next, you're struggling. Honor and disgrace come from God alone. No one achieves greatness or falls into humiliation unless He wills it.

Yes, every time I pass through the desert, each grain of sand, each rise and fall of the landscape, even the mirage on the horizon, walks before my eyes like a patient teacher, imparting its wisdom. And the night sky with its stars ; don't even mention it. The stars shine so brightly and seem so close, as if God Himself has taken them in His hands and is offering them to me, saying: "My son, you are grand and magnificent… you are powerful… you are capable of holding these stars in your hands. One day, you may even discover them and live on one of these beautiful planets. I give these stars to you so you know that whatever you set your mind to, you will surely achieve, for I have breathed My spirit into you. You are My vicegerent on earth, the most noble of My creations."

"Come sit in the shade, sweetheart… What are you staring at?"

"There's so much to see here, Mom… It's beautiful!"

"We pass by here all the time. Why does it always feel new to you, son?"

"Because every time, it teaches me something new."

We had set off early that morning, my family and I, on a bus from Tehran, heading to my hometown of Yazd to visit my grandparents. The city of **windcatchers** and qanats, of traditional architecture and enduring old houses. My father, who had a passion for land and real estate, was planning to buy a piece of land there at a good price. And in the meantime, we were blessed with the opportunity to revisit this magnificent city. Though I had lived there only in the first few years of my life, which I hardly remember, it was still my homeland. Its love was ingrained in my veins and soul without me even realizing it.

"Passengers, please board the bus so we can get going," the driver's voice rang out, bringing relief to everyone as we escaped the heat.

My eyelids began to grow heavy. I pulled my gaze from the window and these beautiful scenes, turned my head to the other side, and let the gentle rocking of the bus lull me to sleep like a cradle. In the row ahead of me sat a tall man with salt-and-pepper hair and an aquiline nose. He had leaned his head back against the seat and had dozed off, still holding the newspaper he had been reading.

August 11th, 1965…Five Corrupt and Criminal Individuals Executed by Firing Squad …Low Rainfall and Drought Threatening Iran.

These snippets from the previous day's newspaper caught my attention.

Drought… low rainfall… No, drought will never come to Yazd. You could say it might affect any other city, but not Yazd. The city of **devotion, qanats, and frugality** will never succumb to dry years. Even though Yazd is a desert city with hot, dry weather, wherever you look, lush and vibrant trees refresh the eyes and bring vitality to the heart. My grandfather used to say that all of this is due to the nature-loving, kind, and frugal people of the city, who cherish even a drop of water and truly understand the value of trees, even a single green leaf.

He was right. I've seen it many times myself: municipal workers and even city residents watering trees by hand with a leather waterskin. Where else in Iran; or the world; do you see such a thing? With simple tools, they dig qanats, bringing water up from the earth to their land.

By noon, we reached Yazd. Though my grandfather had passed away, his house remained as it was, in its traditional form. My grandfather had a friend who lived in an old house that we visited each time we came to Yazd. He had bought the house years ago from an old Yazdi family and restored it, all for the love of its windcatcher. A symbol of traditional Iranian architecture. Perhaps one of the reasons I love traveling to Yazd so much is seeing this windcatcher, and others like it. They remind me of how intelligent and wise our ancestors were.

When I gaze at them, I recall Ferdosi's poem, who gifted the world his masterpiece:

"I have laid the foundation of a lofty palace,

Which will be safe from the wind and rain."

You too, dear ancestors! You have left behind such magnificent buildings and windcatchers that people across the world will forever acknowledge your brilliance, and nothing can tarnish the gift of this God-given talent. Your name and fame will endure for eternity.

But why hasn't anyone continued their path? Are we not the children of such people? Does their blood not flow through our veins? Do we not have the same love for our homeland to follow in their footsteps and build something that will bring pride to our country in front of both friends and foes? With a loud voice, I shouted in that grand structure:

"I can… I will continue their path… I will do something that will make my country renowned… I can… I will!"

The echo of my voice bounced back, filling me with even more determination and motivation:

"I will… I will… I will!"

"Who are you following, Ali Asghar?"

I heard my sister's voice from one of the rooms, and a moment later, she, along with my parents, came toward me.

"You haven't answered your sister, son… Whose path are you continuing?" my father asked.

"The path of the one who built this magnificent windcatcher... I want to build something so grand that everyone who sees it will be in awe."

"Why don't you stick to your homework first, my dear brother! Forget about building windcatchers," my sister teased, taking the perfect opportunity to express her frustration with my lack of enthusiasm for schoolwork.

Even though I was only in third grade, the outside world, with its people and their work, always fascinated me more than school. I must admit, though, I was good at math and loved the subject. Even as a child, I had a passion for numbers and calculations. I was curious to see how people earned their income. Whenever my father brought money home, I would help him count it.

Then I heard my mother's voice; a mother who always cared

deeply about my manners, etiquette, and morals, encouraging my big dreams. She was a wise and capable woman:
"Why do you want to discourage your brother, dear? Mashallah, sweetheart, anything you set your heart on and work hard for, you'll surely achieve."
A little later, my father affectionately patted my head and said:
"Good for you, my son, for having big thoughts and big goals… Just always remember, son, never let anger or frustration lead you to harm. Good character will get you anything you want."
"She's right, son... Don't be like your father was in his youth," my mother added.
My father shot her a sharp glance and, with a scowl, said:
"Enough, woman! Stop bringing up the past... It's a good thing we weren't married back then, or you would've never let that incident go."
What changed my father so profoundly?
What kind of experience had he gone through that now made him so passionately urge me not to repeat his mistakes? I couldn't hold it in anymore, so I asked:
"What memory, Dad? What happened?"
"Nothing, son! Whatever it was, it's over now."
But no, the wound my father had suffered in his youth hadn't healed. It was still fresh, reopened by time. Yet, he wasn't willing to talk about it, so I let it go. Either way, I knew I had to learn from his experience. I had to be kind and courteous, not grumpy and ill-tempered, so people wouldn't distance themselves from me. After all, who doesn't understand the importance of this

principle?

The sound of my younger brother crying reached me from outside the wind tower. Perhaps he had fallen from the two or three steps at the building's entrance. He had a habit of screaming over the smallest accidents. My sister and mother hurried towards him, but it couldn't have been anything serious, as my father stayed behind. He stood in the middle of the wind tower, gazing upwards. A gentle, cool breeze caressed his face, playfully tossing his thinning hair. As he continued staring up, he said:

"Did you know, son, that there used to be a qanat under this building? In the heat, it really helped cool the air inside."

"Yeah, I've heard about it, but I don't really know how it worked."

"Look, wind would enter the building from the top of the wind tower, then reach the lower rooms and basement... The breeze, after passing over the cool waters of the qanat, would return to the building, cooling it down significantly."

"How fascinating! They were so clever!"

The Tutoring Center

I was in fifth grade, and our classroom was on the upper floor of a building on Kerman Street, in the Sara-Asiyab neighborhood of Tehran. Below the stairs of the building was a small shop where a vendor named Mahmoud sold lemons off his three-wheeler. Every day, I'd ask him questions like, "How much do you buy your lemons for? How much do you sell them for? How much do you charge for juicing them? And how much does a bottle of lemon juice cost?"

That day, Mahmoud brought in another load of lemons on his motorbike. He wiped the sweat from his forehead with a handkerchief, then carried three sacks of lemons into his little shop, one by one. Three people stood watching him, waiting to be the first to buy the fresh lemons. Soon, Mahmoud and the others disappeared from my view, drawn inside by the smell of the fresh lemons.

"Ali-Asghar, where's your mind at? What are you looking at?"

"Nothing, teacher!... Sorry."

Our class was on the second floor, and I had seen this scene countless times: Mahmoud unloading his fresh lemons, and people gathering at his shop to buy them. Mahmoud knew me well by now. I was the twelve-year-old who stopped by his shop every day, even if just to say hello. After class, my friend Hassan and I went to his shop again. I asked:

"Mr.Mahmoud! How much lemon did you bring today?"

"Two hundred kilos."

"How much did you buy it for, and how much are you selling it for?"

Mahmoud, ever kind, answered all my questions as usual. Sometimes, he'd be amazed at how a twelve-year-old could be so interested in business, offering him useful suggestions and insights.

After School in the Park

After the last bell, Hassan and I went to a park about a hundred meters from school. Hassan was an athlete. He had won first place in regional student athletics competitions several times, and once even took the national title. I admired his determination and hard work. His perseverance was something I looked up to and tried to learn from. While other classmates wasted their time, I'd see him running, training hard. His house was about an hour's walk from school, and according to him, he ran that distance every day.

Hassan taught me that hard work could get you anywhere. You had to nurture your dreams and work hard for them. You shouldn't give up just because you hit a minor obstacle and then spend your life regretting it.

The previous summer, while working on a construction site, Hassan had fallen off a ladder and injured his right leg. One of the bones in his toe had broken. The doctor told him he shouldn't walk for a while, let alone run, so the injury could heal. This was devastating for Hassan, especially since the national athletics competition was just four months away, and he had set his sights on winning. And now, he was being told not to walk, let alone run.

But to everyone's amazement, four months later, Hassan entered the competition; and won first place. The entire school was stunned, from the teachers to the students. When I asked him how he did it, he gave me an answer that I'll carry with me for the rest of my life. He said he had visualized his victory the whole time. Every night before bed, he would imagine himself, with a healed leg, leading the pack and standing proudly on the podium, the medal around his neck. He said he felt the sweetness of that moment deep in his heart. This mindset, he told me, was something he had learned from his older brother, a champion wrestler. His brother, too, had always visualized his dreams and achieved them.

I spent most of my time with Hassan and other successful friends like him, hoping to become like them one day. My grandmother used to say: "Son, if you want to know someone, look at their friends. A person becomes just like the people they spend the most time with. If you have a hundred good friends and just one bad one, know that the bad one will still influence you and hold you back, even just a little. If you put one diseased goat among a thousand healthy ones, the others will get sick too. So be careful who you befriend."

Our Promise

We finished our homework in the park, spreading out our books and notebooks on the grass. Afterward, we lay down on the lawn, gazing up at the sky.

• "You know, Hassan... Even before I knew about your story of imagining your victories, I used to do that too; without even realizing it."
• "What do you mean?"
• "I've always wanted to build structures that everyone loves, like our ancestors did, like the wind towers in Yazd. They're so

advanced. I dream about it day and night, just like you."
- "That's great! I'm sure you'll achieve it one day... Just remember, never lose hope and always picture your goals in your mind."
- "I will, Hassan! I feel like when God places a dream or goal in our hearts, He's giving us a glimpse of our future. We shouldn't be afraid of having big dreams. I think that even if your dream is as big as owning a planet, if you truly believe in it with all your heart, nothing can stop you from reaching it."
- "Exactly! God has created this world in such a beautiful way... so beautiful! I just don't understand why so many people don't see that."
- "Maybe they once had big dreams too, but over time, they lost hope."
- "Yeah, maybe."
- "Hassan, let's make a promise to ourselves, right here and now, that no matter how hard things get, we'll never give up on our dreams."

We clasped hands and made a pact, vowing that as long as our hearts beat and breath filled our lungs, we would keep pushing towards our goals and never give up.

As we talked, my eyes fell on the cover of Hassan's notebook, where a beautiful verse was written:

"O brother, you are your thoughts.

The rest of you is just bones and sinew."

Below it, the name "Molana" was inscribed, indicating that the poet was Rumi. One of the greatest blessings God had given me; and one I was always grateful for; was that my parents were educated. They introduced me to the works of great scholars, scientists, and poets of Persian literature like Saadi, Hafez, Rumi, and Nizami, as well as scientists like Zakariya al-Razi, Avicenna, Al-Biruni, and Omar Khayyam.

Noticing my gaze, Hassan said:

- "My brother wrote that. He told me it means everything starts in the mind... So always have beautiful thoughts."

I understood the wisdom of that line deeply, and I wrote it in the corner of my own notebook. That was when my love for Rumi's poetry began.

That evening, after leaving the park, I headed home. My parents knew by then that when I stayed out late, it was because I had been with Hassan, either at the park or somewhere else. They weren't worried because they knew I always finished my homework. The scent of my mother's Ghormeh sabzi stew filled the house. Some smells just naturally give you a sense of comfort; like the smell of her stew, the scent of rain-soaked earth, or the warmth of my parents' kindness.

As the sun set, I showed my mother a poem by Rumi and asked her to read the rest to me. Fortunately, we had my grandfather's copy of Rumi's Masnavi at home, along with Golestan and Bustan by Saadi, and Hafez's Divan. My mother, thrilled by my interest in Rumi's poetry, eagerly took the Masnavi book and began to read. After reciting thirty or forty lines, she came to these verses:

"O brother, you are your thoughts, The rest of you is just bones and roots. If your thoughts are like a rose, you are a garden, but if they are thorns, you are firewood for the furnace. If you are like rose water, you will be prized and treasured, but if like urine, you will be cast away. Goodness attracts goodness; it's the rule of the pure."

Rumi's poetry was a bit difficult for me to grasp, so my mother explained it all. She concluded by saying, "The essence of Rumi's words is this: whatever you nurture in your mind will manifest in your life. If your thoughts are like beautiful flowers, you will one day walk in the garden of your dreams. But if your mind is filled with thorns, you will be thrown into the fire of regret and despair, because you will be of no other use. So, it's better to have great and beautiful thoughts, no matter how big; they will surely come true one day."

"How beautiful, Mrs. Anvari... Thank you! Did you knit this yourself?"

"Yes, it's nothing much... We made it in our factory."

"Thank you, Mrs. Anvari... What a lovely gift!... And such intricate knitting!"

The conversation between Mrs. Anvari and my mother woke me from my half-hour afternoon nap. She was a friend of my mother's and owned a textile factory on Lalehzar Street in Tehran, producing all kinds of clothing for men, women, and children. She was likely wearing one of her factory's beautiful creations again, and my mother, as usual, silently admired her colorful clothes, intricate designs, and refined style. Her appearance alone showed her economic status was far better than ours; and rightfully so, given how hard she worked. My mother always spoke highly of her, praising her determination and strength, a woman who ran a factory on her own.

Why not try my hand at this craft, too? Learning this skill could be useful one day. After all, you can't build a grand palace like the wind towers of Yazd with empty hands; you need to work and save up. I think it's a good idea to spend this summer, after my studies and exams are over, working at her factory. I could earn some money and learn a new skill at the same time, just like last summer when I worked alongside Master Mohammad at the construction site and learned new things.

Autumn, winter, and spring passed, and I finished my exams successfully. It was finally time to head to Mrs. Anvari's textile factory and start working. Early one morning, my mother returned from the market with a basket full of fresh herbs and two loaves of Sangak bread. She prepared tea with plain bread, and we gathered to eat. Everyone was there except for my father, who had left for work at the crack of dawn. With kindness, my mother placed cups of tea in front of me, my two sisters, and my brother. I was the middle child in the family. How good it felt to enjoy tea together with fresh Sangak bread.

After breakfast, I helped my sister clear the table and carry the dishes to the kitchen. My mother sat on a chair in the balcony, placed the fresh herbs on the table, and began cleaning them. Without that balcony, I think the house would have felt too confining for her. My father had searched long and hard to find a home in Narmak with a large balcony, big enough for a small table and a few chairs. I sat next to her, helping clean the herbs; fresh parsley, chives, fenugreek, spinach; and thought of how my mother would soon turn them into the tastiest dish in the world.

"Mama, haven't you heard from Mrs. Anvari lately?"

"Why do you ask, my son?"

"I want to learn weaving at her factory."

"What! Weaving? That's not possible, my son."

"Why not, Mama? What's wrong with learning a trade?"

"I didn't say there's anything wrong with it... I just said it's not possible."

"Why?"

"Because Mrs. Anvari closed her factory on Lalehzar and opened a new one in Qazvin."

"That's too bad."

Why hadn't I gone to her factory earlier? Why did I wait until after school to start something new? It's a mistake to postpone one task until another is finished. If I had organized my time better, I wouldn't have these regrets. You always need a plan. Sensing my thoughts, my mother said:

"It's nothing important, my dear! Sure, Mrs. Anvari's factory is gone, but there are plenty of weaving workshops in this city where you can learn the craft."

"You're right, Mama... There's always a way."

Mr. Amiri recalls those days: "When I lost the chance to work at Mrs. Anvari's factory, I started looking for another job. On Lalehzar and Zahir ol-Eslam streets, there was a workshop called Javid, owned by Mr. Arabshahi. That's where I started as an errand boy. Within just four days, I had gained so much attention that Mr. Arabshahi's brother offered me a higher-paying job at their other workshop on Lalehzar and promised to teach me weaving as well.

However, I didn't take that offer because I had set my mind on learning the craft as quickly as possible. To reach my goal, I needed to complete every task given to me in the shortest time and with the highest quality.

The owner was young and recently engaged, so he always wanted to look sharp. Every day, he would send me to the dry cleaner, and I would beg the owner to rush the work so my boss would be satisfied. When I was sent to buy snacks, I had built such a good relationship with the shopkeepers that they would give me the goods and let me pay later, so I wouldn't waste any time. All this made my boss very happy, and within a month, they taught me weaving. I became so skilled that one of the owner's friends, seeing my work, told me I had become a professional and offered me a weaving machine to work at his workshop. But his place was in Bozorgmehr, far from my night school on Lalehzar, so I had to decline."

I learned an important lesson from the experience with Mrs. Anvari's weaving workshop.

If I could plan properly, I knew I'd be able to juggle multiple things at once. School was important, but I also needed to pick up a trade. I didn't want to finish my education only to be left with nothing practical in my hands; no experience, no skills.

The next day, I went looking around the city. I asked around until I finally found a weaving workshop on the second floor of a tall building. I climbed the stairs, and as soon as I entered, I saw people everywhere; busy, working, not paying any attention to a twelve-year-old wandering in. Some were cutting fabric, others managing the machines, and a few were busy sewing. The machines roared so loudly; you couldn't even hear yourself think.

It was hot; so hot that everyone was drenched in sweat. A middle-aged man was moving between the workers, supervising. The noise was so overwhelming that he had to use hand signals to communicate, sometimes with a frown, sometimes with a smile.

The fabrics were incredible; so many colors, so many patterns. I'd never seen anything like it before. I spotted one with white and red flowers, the kind my mom would love. If she saw it, she'd probably stop raving about Mrs. Anvari's factory clothes. Another one caught my eye, too; a blue-striped fabric. I was sure I'd seen it before. Yes! It was the same one my English teacher, Mr. Alborzi, wore in class. So, he was wearing something made right here!

Suddenly, I felt a hand on my shoulder. I turned around to see the man, probably the manager, standing there. He pointed to the weaving machine next to me and shouted, "What are you doing here, kid? Watch your hands around the machines! Who are you?"

What could I say? If I told him I was here for work, he'd probably just laugh and show me out. But if only he could see past my age, if only he could see my dreams. I wasn't skilled in weaving yet, but I could do the little things no one else wanted to do. Just give me a chance!

"Well? What are you doing here?" he asked again.

"I came to work, sir," I replied.

"Have you worked in weaving before?"

"No, but I can be an assistant. I'll do any task you need."

He looked at me thoughtfully and gestured for me to follow him. He led me to a small office at the corner of the workshop. The noise from the machines faded as we closed the door. I had guessed right; he was the manager.

He had such a kind, gentle face. I knew right then that he wouldn't turn me away. Before I knew it, I was telling him everything; about my father, my school, where I lived. It was like I had known him forever. He reminded me of Mr. Tayebi, my father's best friend; warm, understanding, and easy to talk to.

"Why come all the way here from Narmak for simple tasks? Surely, you could've found work as a helper closer to home," he said.

He was right. I needed to tell the truth. His kindness had made me bolder, so I replied, "Honestly, sir, I want to learn weaving. But I'm happy to run errands and do whatever work you need.

Just let me learn the trade while I'm here."

The manager smiled and offered me a chocolate from the box on his desk. I took one, but I was so thirsty I didn't eat it. He didn't chew his either, just let it melt slowly in his mouth, like my grandmother used to do.

"Alright, kid," he finally said, smiling. "You can work here. There's plenty for you to do."

Even though I was almost certain that Hajji wouldn't reject my request, hearing it directly from him filled my heart with light and joy.

"Hajji! Along with those tasks, will you let me learn how to weave and work with the machines as well?"

"Yes, my boy. If you promise to do all your work well, we will definitely teach you weaving, too."

"Thank you! I promise."

"And I promise that you'll become a skilled weaver in this workshop... I'll even pay you a wage every month. Now, get up and start your work from now."

I was expecting him to send me out of the workshop to run errands or fetch some bread, but instead, I saw him reach for the pitcher on the other table, where there were several glasses, and he said, "Go pour yourself a glass of water from that pitcher... It's clear you're very thirsty."

My lips were so dry that anyone could see how desperately thirsty I was. Without hesitation, I walked over to the table. The pitcher was filled with small and large ice cubes, and the water was so cold and refreshing that it felt like the most delicious water I had ever tasted in my life.

From that day, I started my work at the workshop. Hajji turned out to be one of the best people I've ever met in my life. I always prayed that God would place great and successful people in my path.

Days passed by quickly, and now it's been two years that I've been working in this workshop alongside my studies. I not only do the manual labor, but I've also started weaving myself. I worked day and night, learning to value every penny I earned from my hard work, saving up to pursue my bigger dreams in the future.

Hajji was very pleased with me. I completed all the side tasks in record time, so I could focus on the real goal; learning the craft of weaving. Whenever I went downstairs to buy ice, I would rush up the steps two at a time to save every possible moment. Mohsen, who sold ice on the ground floor, became familiar with me as I quickly grabbed the ice and sprinted back to the workshop, often before anyone could notice. I never waited for the change or argued about money. "Next time I come, we'll settle it," I'd say. Time was that precious to me; I treated every second as though it were gold. I truly believed that life is an opportunity God gives us, and we should make the most of it. We can live beautifully if we recognize our worth, our potential, and the grand opportunities life offers.

In these years, I mastered the techniques of weaving. Although most of the people around me were kind and supportive, there's always that one person; someone who, like a thorn, tries to hinder you, to make you question your efforts. For me, that person was Morteza, a boy five years older than me. He was a distant relative of Hajji. In the beginning, when he thought I was just there to do menial tasks, he treated me normally. But once he saw my dedication, my hard work, and how much respect I gained from Hajji, he began making my life difficult. The more kindness I showed him, the more hostility he displayed. It felt like I was pouring water on a rock, trying to soften it. The old saying, "Jealousy burns the jealous," became so real to me. He was like a watchful camera, constantly zooming in on me, hoping to catch any mistake so he could exaggerate it and report it to Hajji. But he found nothing; no matter how hard he looked, he found nothing wrong. And that only made him angrier.

One day, when Hajji was absent, he had entrusted me to oversee the workers and monitor the machines. Everything was going smoothly until one of the workers came and told me someone was looking for me. When I stepped outside, I saw a young man, clearly ravaged by addiction. His body was thin and weak, his teeth yellowed with a few missing, and his clothes were tattered and dirty. The stench of cigarettes and who knows what else clung to him. I wondered why someone like him would have business with me. Then he spoke, claiming he had a message from my father. He said my father had been in an accident and was taken to the hospital in bad shape. He even gave me the hospital address and urged me to go there quickly.

My legs felt weak, and my heart pounded as fear gripped me. I was about to rush out to the hospital when something inside me hesitated. I decided to call my father's workplace first, which I had memorized. I ran to Hajji's office, which he had entrusted me with the keys to, and made the call. No one answered the first two times, and my anxiety only grew. But on the third attempt, someone picked up, and I asked for my father. There was a moment of silence, then I heard my father's voice on the other end.

"Hello? Who's this?"

It was like pouring water on a fire; my panic subsided immediately. "Hello, Dad."

"Ali Asghar, is that you? Why are you calling in the middle of the day? Is something wrong?"

"No, Dad... I just wanted to hear your voice."

"Oh... Is that all? Are you okay?"

"Yes, I'm fine. Is everything alright with you? Alright then, goodbye."

I hung up before he could ask more questions. I didn't want to waste any time. I rushed back out, ready to confront that lying addict, but he was nowhere to be found. Who was he, and why did he make up such a story? Strange people in this world... But thank God my father was fine. That was all that mattered to me. I quickly made my way back to the machines. Hajji had trusted me to manage things today, after all. As I approached, I noticed that the usual noise of the workshop had quieted down. I could hear the workers talking clearly near the machine. It had stopped running. When I asked what happened, they told me the machine had broken down a few minutes ago and no one could get it working again.

What was I supposed to tell Hajji? He had run this workshop flawlessly for forty years, and now, on the very day he put me in charge, everything fell apart. Should I tell him I wasn't worthy of the trust he placed in me? That I wasn't cut out to be a leader? Before Hajji returned, I had to fix this. I approached Mr. Ali, one of the older and more experienced workers, and asked him to take a look at the machine. But after some effort, he couldn't figure out the problem either. The best help he offered was giving me the contact information for Mr. Tavakoli, a repairman who specialized in these kinds of machines.

I quickly ran back to Hajji's office and called Mr. Tavakoli, begging him to come to the workshop as soon as possible. At first, he said he was too busy, but after I insisted, he agreed to be there in an hour. I prayed that Hajji wouldn't return before then. I couldn't bear to let him down.

Finally, Mr. Tavakoli arrived, and I quickly took him to the broken machine. Within less than five minutes, he identified the problem; a part was missing. He looked around but couldn't find it. He said he would go back to his workshop and bring the part the next morning to fix the machine. However, tomorrow would be too late. Even a minute more was too late. What if Hajji suddenly showed up? I insisted, and luckily, Mr. Tavakoli was kind enough to understand my anxiety. It was as if he could read my mind and feel my desperation. He decided to call his shop from there. We went back to Hajji's office, and Mr. Tavakoli dialed the number. His assistant answered, and within thirty minutes, the part was delivered to the workshop. Mr. Tavakoli fixed the machine in no time, and soon the familiar hum filled the space again; it was even running better than before. Everything returned to normal, and the workers resumed their tasks. I paid for the repair and the service out of my own pocket, but it was worth every penny. Maintaining Hajji's trust and not failing in my responsibility was invaluable.

Hajji arrived at the workshop later that afternoon, and I was relieved to see that he was satisfied with my work. The events of that day still felt suspicious; the young man's presence in the workshop, his lies, and Mortaza's nervous face lingering around the machine. Yet, there was no concrete evidence to prove that anyone had tampered with the equipment. I decided to calm my mind and chalk it up to an accident. The most important thing was that everything had returned to normal, but I knew I had to be more vigilant from now on.

However, the story didn't end there. Early the next morning, Hajji summoned me to his office. With his usual warm smile, he asked, "Did anything happen yesterday, Ali?"

I hesitated, "What do you mean?"

"Mortaza mentioned the machine broke down."

"It was nothing, Hajji, just a minor issue. It's fixed now."

"Mortaza also said that Mr. Tavakoli, the repairman, came by. Is that right?"

At that moment, Mortaza walked in with a smirk on his face, staring directly into my eyes as he greeted me. I'd never seen him initiate a greeting before.

"You were saying, Ali Asghar?"

"Yeah, Hajji, the machine broke down, so I called Mr. Tavakoli, and he came and fixed it."

Mortaza and I both stood there, waiting for Hajji to lose his temper and say, "I gave you one simple task, and you couldn't handle it! You messed up!" But instead, Hajji reacted in a completely different way. It was as if my respect had grown in his eyes. He smiled at me kindly and said, "Well done, my boy! You've made me proud. Now I can be confident that if I'm ever not around, you'll run this workshop smoothly. You didn't have to go the extra mile, but you did, even paying for the repair yourself. You're responsible and determined, and I'm proud of you."

This added fuel to the fire of Mortaza's jealousy. His face turned red, his sly smile faded into a scowl, and his hands began to tremble. I could see the anger rising inside him, like a volcano about to erupt. If Hajji hadn't been there, Mortaza would have unleashed his fury on me. But instead, he stormed out of the room without a word. His resentment toward me had intensified, and I knew I had to be even more careful and diligent in my work.

One day, while I was cutting fabric with one of the workers, a loud argument erupted. It was Mortaza, fighting with Yadollah, who was in charge of sewing. They were yelling profanities at each other, and even Hajji couldn't calm them down. Apparently, Mortaza had switched his broken sewing machine with

Yadollah's to make it seem like Yadollah was at fault. But Yadollah wasn't someone who would back down easily. He was hot-tempered and blunt. I overheard them shouting during the argument:

"Mortaza, don't make me lose my temper…"

"And what are you going to do about it?" Mortaza spat, gripping Yadollah by the collar.

"Let go of me… Don't make me speak."

"Speak then! What nonsense are you going to spew?"

"Fine, you asked for it."

Yadollah turned to Hajji, who was trying to separate them, and said, "Hajji, when you weren't here the other day, I saw Mortaza tampering with the machine. He removed a part and threw it in the trash. He was trying to sabotage Ali Asghar. I even saw him bring in one of his friends to distract Ali while he messed with the machine. That friend's name is Pouya; he's an addict, and if you give him a bit of money, he'll admit to anything. I swear, Hajji, I saw it with my own eyes!"

The room went silent. Mortaza let go of Yadollah's collar, and Yadollah, having finally let out his pent-up frustration, walked over to his station, placed his sewing machine back on his table, and left Mortaza's broken one on the floor. Mortaza, standing there, ashamed in front of Hajji, had nothing to say. He simply stood with his head bowed.

But Hajji, as if he already knew everything, didn't even raise an eyebrow. He turned to the workers who had gathered and said, "What's going on here? Why are you all standing around? Get back to work!" He then lowered his head and walked back to his office. We all knew, including Mortaza, that Hajji had given him another chance.

Days and months passed. Every day, Mortaza would hatch a new plan against me, but each time I emerged unscathed, ignoring him. One day, I reflected on my situation. When I was younger, my mother used to tell me stories from Kalila and Demna. Demna was a fox who would do anything to rise to power. He was envious and couldn't stand anyone being above him. He didn't want anyone other than himself to have a close relationship with the king of the jungle. So, he schemed to destroy the friendship between the lion and the cow by spreading lies. Eventually, the lion, though good-natured, was poisoned by Demna's words and killed the cow. But in the end, Demna met his own downfall when the truth came to light, and the lion killed him.

I realized that no matter how good Hajji was, Mortaza might one day plant seeds of doubt in his heart about me. There were many other workshops in Tehran. It wasn't that I felt defeated; I had learned everything I needed to know. During my time in the workshop, I had met several other business owners, many of whom were kind and honorable, like Hajji. One of them, Mr. Mohammad Reza Mahdizadeh, had repeatedly invited me to join his workshop, but out of respect for Hajji, I had always declined. However, I had made up my mind. That afternoon, I would speak to Hajji and tell him about my decision.

When the workday was over, I went to Hajji's office and told him I intended to move to Mr. Mahdizadeh's workshop. Hajji, in his calm manner, asked, "You're tired of Mortaza's antics, aren't you?"

"No, Hajji... To be honest, I've learned so much from you. I've told you before that I want to master this craft, and Mr. Mahdizadeh's workshop has some new machines that I think could teach me even more."

"You're right, my boy. His workshop is more advanced, and their products are more up-to-date. I wish you all the success. I'm glad we worked together for these years. I'm sure you have a bright future ahead of you."

And so, my new journey began at a new workshop, and I gained a wealth of new experiences.

Later, I heard from a friend at the old workshop that Hajji had eventually fired Mortaza. Apparently, Mortaza had continued causing problems for the newer workers, costing Hajji a lot of money. Demna had finally met his fate, consumed by his own jealousy.

Working in the textile workshop continued alongside my other jobs. I was doing multiple tasks at once, and eventually, I decided to open my own textile workshop. By the age of sixteen, I had learned everything I needed to know. But how would I afford the machines? And where would I start? One night before bed, I sat down and wrote everything out; the cost of the machines, workers' wages, rent for a place. I wrote it all down because I believed in the power of writing things out. It felt like once you wrote your goals on paper, you had already completed half the journey. Writing brought your vision into reality, making it more achievable.

It was as if you were painting a picture of your future, and every picture would eventually become real. After all, I am the creator of my own life. I am the artist who can paint my future however I want; either beautiful or ugly. So why not paint something beautiful? I am the author who can write either a good or bad story for myself. If someone is aware of the incredible power within them and their ability to shape their life, why would they choose to create anything ugly or unpleasant? That would be the height of madness. Writing, to me, is a tool for creating the world you want. It's no coincidence that God swore by the pen in the Quran's Surah al-Qalam (The Pen). Writing is magic.

It feels like when you write down the future you envision, you send out vibrations of possibility into the universe. Everyone around you starts to admire and affirm your work, goals, and dreams, and new, positive ideas begin to flow into your mind. It's as if you've taken a step forward, and another step follows naturally, guiding you forward step by step. But as long as those thoughts remain only in your mind and unwritten, neither you nor anyone else can validate them, leaving them forever out of reach.

My entire investment was two hundred meters of land that I had purchased last year with my earnings as a laborer while working in a weaving workshop. I had to sell it. I needed to let go of this small pleasure to experience a greater one. This decision had

become easier for me. When I was a child, my mother taught me a game to help my siblings and me understand that if we could pass up immediate, fleeting pleasures, we would achieve much greater joys. Every Friday when we visited my older sister's house, she would take my siblings and me into a room and place a chocolate bar in front of each of us. Then she would say:
"I'm going to make some tea for Mom and Dad. Anyone who hasn't touched their chocolate by the time I get back will receive three chocolates instead of just one."
It feels as if, when you write down the future you envision, you send out ripples of possibility into the universe. Everyone around you starts to admire and validate your work, dreams, and goals, while fresh, positive ideas begin to flow into your mind. It's as if you've taken a step forward, and another follows naturally, guiding you onward step by step. But as long as those thoughts remain only in your mind and unwritten, neither you nor anyone else can give them validation, leaving them perpetually out of reach.
My entire investment consisted of two hundred meters of land that I had bought last year with my earnings as a laborer in a weaving workshop. I had to sell it. I needed to part with this small pleasure to embrace a greater one. This decision had become easier for me over time. As a child, my mother taught me a game to help my siblings and me understand that by passing up fleeting pleasures, we could achieve much greater joys. Every Friday, when we visited my older sister's house, she would take my siblings and me into a room, placing a chocolate bar in front

of each of us. Then she would say:

"I'm going to make some tea for Mom and Dad. Anyone who hasn't touched their chocolate by the time I return will receive three chocolates instead of just one."

When she left the room, each of us exchanged glances. The temptation to eat the chocolate was overwhelming. The first time, except for my other sister and me, everyone devoured their chocolate. When my sister returned, she gave the two of us three chocolates each. This game repeated every Friday until we learned the lesson well.

Now, it wasn't difficult for me to sell the land I had worked for years to acquire, as it would lead me to the greater pleasure of earning more. I needed to buy the machinery for the weaving workshop with the money from the sale. So, one evening after dinner, when my father went to the park next to our house for his usual half-hour walk, I approached him to discuss my plan to sell the land. However, my father was against it and insisted that I keep the land. I remained firm in my decision until he sat down on one of the benches in the park, and I leaned against it.

"Look, son, never act out of emotion... Whether it's anger, sadness, or fleeting happiness, don't let it lead you to make a decision you'll regret later."

Anger... I recalled a day when my mother revived a memory for my father. He had advised me to always be kind and cheerful and to stay away from anger. That day, he had stayed silent, and now he wanted to speak up, to express everything he hadn't said before. So, I sat quietly and calmly, ready to listen to his words and forever remember my father's bitter experience, which served as a lesson for me.

When she stepped out of the room, we all exchanged glances, the temptation to indulge in the chocolate gnawing at us. The first time we played, except for my other sister and me, everyone devoured their chocolates. When my sister returned, she rewarded the two of us with three chocolates each. This game continued every Friday until we learned the lesson well.

Now, selling the land I had toiled for over the years didn't seem difficult because it would lead me to the greater pleasure of earning more. I needed the proceeds to buy machinery for the weaving workshop. One evening, after dinner, when my father went to the park next to our house for his usual half-hour walk, I approached him to share my plan about selling the land. However, my father opposed the idea and insisted that I hold onto it. I was determined to stick to my decision until he sat down on one of the park benches, and I leaned against it.

"Listen, son, never act out of emotion... Whether it's anger, sadness, or fleeting joy, don't let those feelings push you into a decision you might regret later."

Anger... I was reminded of a day when my mother revived a memory for my father. He had once advised me to always be kind and cheerful, steering clear of anger. That day, he had remained silent, and now he felt compelled to speak, to express everything he had kept to himself. So, I sat quietly, ready to absorb his words, eager to learn from his bitter experiences that would forever serve as valuable lessons for me.

Back in my youth, filled with the pride and impulsiveness characteristic of those years, before marrying your mother, a few fellow Yazdis and I moved to Tehran to start a real estate agency in Sabzeh Meydan. Over the years, I managed to acquire a considerable amount of land in Vali-Asr and Bahjatabad. I was hard-working, determined, and capable; everything in my life seemed to be falling into place. However, I had one major flaw: I would get angry too quickly, leading me to make impulsive decisions that resulted in significant losses.

During my peak in real estate, I found myself in need of some money and approached my father for help. Unfortunately, he couldn't provide even the small amount I needed at that time. I mistakenly thought he didn't want to assist me, which fueled my anger. In a fit of rage, I lost all the lands I had worked so hard to acquire overnight. I sold everything below market value and left for Khuzestan to seek work. All this loss stemmed from acting on my emotions and anger; if only I had controlled my feelings, I would now own numerous properties and perhaps even have started a business for you.

My father was concerned that I might be selling the land out of ignorance, thinking I was acting on impulse. However, once I shared my intentions with him, he agreed to the sale but insisted that I promise to buy another piece of land. If he hadn't emphasized this, I would have certainly purchased land once I earned some income.

From the sale of the land, I received eight thousand tomans, which I used to buy machinery. To avoid paying rent for a workspace, I decided to convert our basement into a workshop. I organized the space, purchased the machines, and became my own boss in the weaving workshop.

One day while I was deeply engaged in my work, Mr. Fakhari's brother; the buyer of my land; visited our home. He saw how absorbed I was in my tasks, to the point that I didn't even have time to greet him. He remarked, "It's clear you will succeed because you plan every second of your time in your workshop and in life. I have a place on Khorasan Street that I can rent to you." Hearing this made me incredibly happy, and I eagerly agreed. I then welcomed him and discussed the weaving and finishing of garments, explaining that these products resembled a bountiful harvest completed through skillful craftsmanship. I asked him to choose some as gifts. He accepted my offering, and together we went to see the proposed location, which I took over.

Things progressed remarkably well. After several months of good income, I used the money to purchase new machines and equipment. I added a couple of workers to the workshop, and within two to three years, I was able to buy another piece of land and began constructing on it. I also expanded the production workshop and, along with a friend, purchased a shop. None of this would have been possible if I hadn't worked over 22 hours a day. Even while sleeping, my mind was busy; when my mother would call me to go to work, I'd reply in my sleep, "Wait, Mom, I still need to knit a few more sleeves."

In construction projects, I worked personally alongside the foreman and the builders. This had several advantages: I learned the craft well because I had a lofty goal; to create beautiful buildings. Additionally, I saved on some costs by working as hard as two or three workers, and finally, I could oversee everything closely.

In this way, God elevated my work at every stage and placed good people along my path to help me achieve my dreams. At my new workshop, blessings flowed abundantly, and everything progressed according to my plans. I encountered new people, each offering valuable lessons, and their suggestions and opinions mattered to me.

I derived immense joy from learning new things. I aspired to have multiple sources of income, so I evaluated every new venture carefully before trying it out. I knew that these lessons would eventually prove beneficial and open new doors. Perhaps this drive came from my grandfather, my father's father, Abdul Razzaq.

I had heard from my father that he, although a khan, always engaged in specific and economical endeavors that perhaps ordinary people's minds couldn't fathom. He was very opportunistic and made excellent use of opportunities.

Father said that once, due to low rainfall, plants, grass, and agricultural products suffered damage, which in turn harmed livestock owners and farmers in his city, where the primary professions were livestock breeding and agriculture. He took advantage of this situation by hiring a group of individuals who engaged in trading livestock. Because of the drought and lack of grazing land, livestock in Yazd held little value. However, in regions where rainfall was plentiful, the worth of these animals was significant. Thus, he would purchase livestock at a low price in Yazd and transport them to a fertile area like Fars, where he could sell them for a good profit. This venture brought considerable earnings to my grandfather. This was one of his wise and calculated actions, a legacy of his prudence that has also been passed down to me.

Downstairs, there was a man named Abolfazl who ran a workshop repairing various electrical and household appliances. Occasionally, he also created tools and gadgets. One of his inventions was three-wheeled motors designed for disabled individuals. I often visited his shop during my free time, observing his meticulous work until I learned how to construct these vehicles myself.

One day, as I was heading to my workshop, I saw him sitting in front of his store. Upon seeing me, he stood up and greeted me warmly. As always, I shook his hand enthusiastically and responded with a friendly smile. As I was climbing the first step, he called out to me and said:

"Mr. Amiri, do you have a moment to talk?"

"Yes, of course... Is something wrong?"

"No, there's no problem... I wanted to discuss work with you."

"Go ahead, Mr. Abolfazl... I'm all ears."

He led me into the store, filled two cups with tea, and said, "There's a company across the street, just past the bank... Have you seen it?"

"Yes, I've seen it... What about it?"

"Recently, one of their employees came to the shop and mentioned that he heard you make three-wheelers for the disabled... He asked me to produce a large number for them, offering good pay."

"Okay..."

"To be honest, I don't have enough capital to purchase the raw materials... I noticed that you also enjoy this work... If it's possible, we could partner in this endeavor... You provide the investment, and I'll handle the work."

Whenever I received a job offer or wanted to engage in a new venture, I would carefully assess all aspects of it in my mind, with the main criteria being whether it would bring me profit and whether it was ethical and would not violate anyone's rights. Long ago, I had simplified my decision-making process by writing down all my criteria in one of my notebooks. I refer to "notebooks" because I maintain special notebooks for many of my affairs, recording accounts, profits, losses, purchases, sales, and my expectations. In that moment, even without a notebook in front of me, I remembered all my criteria.

"Alright... I'll definitely invest, and since I learned this work myself, I can also help with the construction alongside you."

He was delighted by my affirmative response. We agreed to meet again in the afternoon to discuss the preliminary steps for starting the project and to create a list of all the necessary materials for constructing the three-wheelers.

That meeting took place, and we initiated the project, resolving some issues for several disabled individuals while also earning a significant profit from the venture.

In 1978, the country was engulfed in turmoil and changes. Everywhere there was noise and conflict. No businesses were thriving; all the shops were closed. The streets became arenas for protests and clashes, and with my workshop and construction projects halted, I joined the ranks of the revolutionaries. Eventually, the revolution succeeded, but due to the changes that took place, the economic situation had not yet stabilized. Inflation was rampant. The borders were open, allowing goods, clothing, and fabric to flood the country. Previously, due to my credibility, I used to buy the raw materials for my weaving workshop for 34,000 tomans and sell them the following year at the same price without any price increases. However, now things had changed. No matter how much credit I had, I couldn't purchase goods at a fixed price, as inflation had taken hold everywhere. I had to improve the quality of my work and increase production to compensate for the losses.

However, I never stopped working even for a moment. Once, I had read a saying from one of the Imams. He saw a man whose business had declined and who spent his days idly. The Imam asked him why he was wasting his time, to which the man replied that he had no capital to buy goods. The Imam advised him to open his shop, place a few containers of water in it, and sell the water. The man followed this advice, and soon his business returned to normal, allowing him to stock his shop again and sell goods.

This Imam's suggestion contained profound wisdom. Everything begins from within a person. If you envision success in your profession and business, the universe aligns itself to make it happen. If you strive and believe you will achieve your goals, it will certainly be so.

I faced many obstacles but persevered. During that time, I owned twelve villas. The Minister of Housing stated that no villas should be constructed, even as housing prices plummeted, leaving me no choice but to sell. Losses... losses... For years, I paid a monthly installment of six thousand tomans. Yet, I didn't let it consume my thoughts or wallow in negative feelings. I knew that one day these losses would be compensated. Housing prices eventually rose again, allowing me to buy land and start construction. Over time, the building and weaving sectors stabilized. I worked tirelessly, wasting not a second of my time, and amid the post-revolutionary circumstances, I managed to buy a Benz.

Indeed, I strove in those conditions, had faith and belief, practiced patience and reliance, and hoped that everything would turn out in my favor. I knew that no external event could hinder my progress if my inner self remained calm and free from external worries. I had learned not to regard difficulties and obstacles as limitations but rather as opportunities or experiences God placed in my path for my growth. To me, every hardship and problem leads a person toward a higher state of perfection.

It is not without reason that the Quran states, "Indeed, with hardship comes ease." Yet, alas... it is a shame that most people are unaware of this important principle. My spirit and soul have become intertwined with the poetry of Rumi. Only he and a few others like him regard difficulties as sweet as honey. If God were to rescue them from these hardships, they would lament because they have realized that from the depths of swamps, a lotus always emerges. Who, like this accomplished mystic, perceives afflictions, fire, and torment as blessings and light? Who speaks in solitude with their Creator like this?

Your cruelty is better than any fortune;

Your revenge is dearer to my soul.

Is this your fire, or is this your light?

This lamentation, what form does it take?

Among the sweetness, your injustice abounds,

And no one knows the depth of your grace.

I lament, fearing that he may believe

That, by His grace, I deserve less of your cruelty.

By God, if I become a thorn in the garden,

I will lament like the nightingale for this reason.

I love him for both his kindness and his wrath;

What a wonder; I am in love with both these opposites.

War... unrest... the thirst for power... violence... It seems the world will never be free from these evils. Since the dawn of creation, from the day Cain's hands were stained with his brother's blood to the moment Joseph fell into the well of jealousy and hatred at the hands of his brothers, the world has been plagued by these dark shadows. It was on the day when the first bullets shattered the peace of the birds hidden among the trees that the flames of hatred, jealousy, and the desire for power ignited in people's hearts. There always seem to be humans who cannot bear to see the world in joy, so they create chaos and rebellion, seeking to turn the world into the turbulent reflection of their own troubled souls. In this struggle, some must sacrifice themselves, standing firm with their lives to protect even a speck of their homeland from being taken. Our homeland has not lacked these valiant men; those who took their lives into their hands and marched to the battlefield. They fought and fell.

Around three o'clock on the last day of September 1980, as the sonic barrier broke over Tehran, we climbed to the roof of the new factory on the crossroads of Jomhoori. After hearing the sirens from the radio, suddenly, the voice of Mr. Khamenei echoed, declaring that the forces of Saddam and the Ba'ath Party of Iraq had violated Iran's air and land borders, and that we would respond to this aggression. He urged the great nation of Iran to remain steadfast.

A wave of chatter enveloped the workshop. Everyone paused from their work, inquiring about what had transpired. That day, I closed the workshop earlier than usual and returned home. Days passed, and every street and alley witnessed mothers bidding farewell to their children as they stepped forward to defend their homeland. Young and old were present, but the courage of the youth stood out; the true warriors of the battlefield, not the streets.

It was a bleak evening. My mother sat on the balcony, murmuring under her breath: "Oh God, help them... God, protect these young lives... God, safeguard our homeland." Her heart ached, yearning for the young men who left the city every day, eager to become guardians of their people. If she heard that her son intended to join the front lines, her heart would be in turmoil. Could she, like other mothers, bear to sacrifice her child for the homeland?

"Hello, Mother."

"Hello, my son... When did you arrive? I called the workshop, and they said you weren't there."

"Yes, Mother! I wasn't there. I went to see Ali and Hassan to discuss going to the front, and now I've come to inform you and Father of this matter to seek your permission."

I shared everything with her. She fell into deep thought. She must have suspected she would soon hear this news from me. Thus, her response was ready. She had things to say; things that resonated with logic and made sense to me. She said that defending our homeland is not just about fighting. Do these brave men heading to the front lines not need anything for a successful battle? Are there not cold and harsh autumn and winter months approaching? Who will prepare their uniforms? How can one fight valiantly without warm clothing?

"Oh, Mother! Your fear of losing your child has led you to think wisely."

So, the next day, I began preparing and sewing uniforms for the soldiers. The sounds of the workshop grew louder every day. I poured my heart and soul into my work, as if I wanted to contribute to the defense of my homeland. Trucks filled with uniforms, especially warm winter clothing, flowed from my workshop to the battlefront.

Once, when we sent trucks loaded with uniforms to the front, I joined a group of engineers to the naval forces in Bushehr. It was the day when the destroyer "Peykan" was attacked by the Iraqis, resulting in the martyrdom of Commander Mohamad Ibrahim Hemmati. We were busy repairing the "Gorz" and "Tabarzin" destroyers.

At that time, I heard that a fierce operation was underway between our naval forces and the Iraqi forces; the "Pearl Battle." Saddam aimed to destroy the Iranian navy, but such a thought was utterly mistaken. He had not yet recognized the bravery and courage of the heroes of my homeland.

About ten or twelve destroyers had been built for Iran in France and had recently arrived in the country. One of these destroyers was named "Peykan," commanded by Mohamad Ibrahim Hemmati; a brave warrior with around 130 crew members, fighting valiantly at sea. However, a problem arose with the destroyer. The steam generator had broken down, a catastrophe for forces who might be engaged in battle at sea for a month or more. One of the functions of this generator was cooking food for the troops. If it failed, it would create a significant disruption in their ability to fight.

At that moment, God had sent me to the front to apply the knowledge I had learned professionally to solve this problem; a knowledge gained from my time with Abolfazl. So, we set off for Bushehr, joining the engineering team. The heat in Bushehr was unbearable, as if the sun had descended to the earth to witness the war up close and admire the brave soldiers.

My mother was right: not everything is about fighting. Other services can be provided as well. I need to heal the wounds marked on the body of the ship "Peykan," which has sent several Iraqi vessels to the depths of the Persian Gulf, thanks to Commander Hemmati. I have to take a small step for Commander Hemmati, who has thwarted Iraq's oil exports through the Persian Gulf and the Sea of Oman by setting fire to the oil terminals of Al-Bakr and Al-Amaya. In comparison to the bravery of the warriors, my efforts seem trivial, akin to bringing cumin to Kerman or a grasshopper's leg to Solomon. Yet, I ask you, my homeland, to accept this humble gift of mine:

"Oh king, a gift to you with a hundred lives is less than bringing cumin to Kerman, yet you know that it is the way of ants to bring a grasshopper's leg to Solomon."

We began the repair work on the generator. I checked every part to identify the problem. Alas, the makers of this generator designed it in such a way that if the slightest issue arises, you have only two options: either replace it and buy a new generator from them or have it repaired solely by them and not by local forces. They make simple tasks so complicated that we are forever reaching out to them for help.

Each component of this boiler operated on a different voltage. They weren't the same; if the burner failed, it wouldn't work with the voltages of the other parts. If the exhaust or switch malfunctioned, you had to replace or repair the entire boiler. I didn't have much expertise, so I quickly began reading articles about this type of equipment. Eventually, I managed to set all the components to operate on 220 volts, completely eliminating the problem at its core. Now, if any part encounters an issue, it won't require the manufacturers' specialists, and local teams can easily repair it.

Once again, the heroic Peykan plunged into the sea. The commander and his forces aimed to instill fear in the enemies and strike their hearts. Again, with its missiles, it sank several Iraqi vessels to the ocean floor. However, just at the last moments when its missiles ran out, the Iraqis hit it. Peykan sank, and Commander Hemmati and his comrades ascended to the heavens.

It is said that in part of his will, Commander Hemmati wrote that if even a speck of my homeland's soil sticks to the boots of the enemy soldier, I will wash it with my blood in the homeland, and I consider death in this cause an honor. If I had a gift more valuable than my life, I would surely present it to these good people.

Indeed, Commander Hemmati achieved the lofty rank of martyrdom on December 7, 1980, during Operation Pearl, one of the largest operations of the Navy of the Army.

After the sinking of the vessel, I had to return to Tehran to procure more clothing for the warriors. Bushehr had fallen into a deep sleep. The city was silent, and the factories were still and quiet. The sun's rays streamed down, causing sweat to flow from our brows. There were no vehicles to take us to the main road, so we set out on foot in the sweltering heat. Not a single shadow in sight to perhaps rest under and escape those scorching rays. But I found one... a hundred meters ahead, I spotted a cow. I walked and walked until I reached that small shadow; a black cow with a white crescent on its forehead; a moon of a forehead. The terror of war had stripped this poor cow of its flesh. It was nothing more than a skeleton, and I rested for a moment in the shade of this bony creature. The cow was as thirsty as my water bottles. I gently patted its head and said, "Oh gentle cow, don't worry... the dreadful and ominous days of war will depart from this country, and you will graze freely in the meadows once again; you will grow plump again."

I needed to reach the main road more quickly. Night was approaching. The weaving workshop awaited me. The soldiers' uniforms... By the way, I haven't forgotten about you, beautiful buildings, from whose windows one can gaze at a city filled with security and peace, far from war. The sprouts of constructing you still live in my heart, but please wait a little. Today, I have an important task and a significant duty on my shoulders. Wait until my country finds peace.

Peace and tranquility have settled over the country. Many young lives were lost, mothers mourned, fathers ascended to the skies, and many saw the grief of their beloved children, but all this blood bore fruit; the soil of the homeland was not plundered. The sounds of laughter and joy from children echoed in the streets once more.

At the end of the war in 1988, we moved to America, to the city of Boston. A few of my Iranian and American friends lived in this city. Shahrokh was one of them, and we explored the entire city together until our journey brought us to the riverbank. How beautiful and charming it was! How amazing it would be to build a lovely hotel on the other side of the river. Why hasn't anyone built such a hotel yet? Why are there so few hotels in Boston? Why are the most important needs of tourists overlooked in such an advanced city?

"What's on your mind, Ali Asghar? What are you thinking about?"

"Did you see that place? The one across the river with the building that has a pink roof?"

"Yeah, I saw it... So?"

"That's a perfect spot for a hotel... you don't know what a view it has... it would be unparalleled."

"Really? You think you can build such a beautiful hotel?"

"Of course, I can... I can already imagine what it looks like in my mind."

Shahrokh fell silent for a moment. He ran a hand over his head and murmured under his breath, "Dr. Farhadi." Then he said aloud:

"Dr. Farhadi."

"Who is Dr. Farhadi?"

"He's someone who can help you build the hotel you want there."

"And who is this Mr. Farhadi that has such power in another country?"

"He's my friend... the legal deputy of the governor of Boston."
"Really?"
"Yeah... I'll definitely call him tomorrow and discuss this with him, then let you know."
That night, the phone at the hotel rang. I heard Shahrokh's voice:
"Hello. Ali Asghar."
"Hi Shahrokh, how are you?"
"I talked to Farhadi."
"So?"
"It seems like it's been a long time coming for him... Farhadi said he has been wanting to build a beautiful hotel in this city in that location for a long time, and he said that someone with such a vision can surely do a great job because I've been thinking about it for fifteen years."
"What's the plan now?"
"Farhadi wants to have a meeting tomorrow at two so that the governor can discuss this with you."
"How wonderful... absolutely."
"Just don't forget... tomorrow at two at the governor's office."
"Sure... definitely."
The next day, I was at the governor's office right at two o'clock. The meeting was held promptly, and discussions took place. My ideas resonated well with the governor. He had a vision for such a project and seemed to be waiting for someone to come along and show him the location and put it into action. He had been looking for someone to execute this vision and was so pleased with this proposal that if he could speak Persian, he would have

said, "The water is in the jug, and we are wandering the world. You are here, and I'm constantly looking for someone to realize my vague ideas."

One or two more meetings were held, but as this project progressed, doubts crept into my heart. What are you doing, Ali Asghar? You have nurtured a lifetime of dreams and goals in your heart and mind, and now you want to realize them in a foreign land? You've looked at every corner of Iran, searching for the perfect place to build your dream palace, and now you're searching for it somewhere else? Isn't there enough scenery and nature in your homeland? Don't your people deserve a small service from you? No... I will never do this except for my country... I withdrew from this project... and quickly informed Shahrokh of my decision. I was painfully reminiscent of India; I thought of my homeland. My love for my country took hold of me. I must return to Iran.

After returning from the United States, I dedicated myself once again to hard work and effort. Years later, I found myself in Astara, heading to a place I had envisioned many times in my solitude. I had often imagined the very first building I would construct here. If you were to ask the individual drops of seawater or each leaf on the trees of this forest, they would testify to the whispers of a young man who promised to one day come and paint his canvas of dreams right under this clear blue sky, beside the lush trees and the endless sea. It was the day when he would have saved enough capital, when his hands would be full, when the time for the fruits of his relentless efforts had finally arrived.

Yes, I had visited this beautiful nature many times, but what could I do when my hands weren't as full as they should have been? Now, however, they were overflowing. I worked day and night until my pockets were sufficiently full to realize all that I wanted. I had lived a life of simplicity since childhood, and I considered this to be the greatest wealth I had always possessed. I let go of my small joys, setting aside my trivial and fleeting desires to build my grand palace of dreams. The game nights spent at my sister's house were yielding results, nearing completion. I had sacrificed a small piece of chocolate so that the flavor of many chocolates would now sweeten the lives of myself and others. Yes, one must practice moderation, but not to the extent of closing one's hand against generosity or becoming miserly. If one were to look at narratives or Quranic verses, everything is laid out; God advises not to keep your hand tightly closed when doing good to others, nor to open it so widely that you end up in blame and despair.

When observing the lives of great and wealthy individuals, it's clear that they always share part of their wealth with others because they understand its secret and wisdom. They know this act attracts even more abundance towards them. It's as if by sharing your wealth, you are telling the world, "Look at me, how rich and fortunate I am, so rich that I can extend my hand to others." Thus, I deserve abundance, deserving of more, so give me more; more wealth, more kindness, more humanity; because I am worthy of it.

I needed to implement this decision as soon as possible. It seemed as though God had inspired me that this was the best time to achieve my goals, and I shouldn't delay, not even for a second. I have always believed that starting a task well today is better than beginning it excellently tomorrow. One must take action, make a mark, so that the mind doesn't keep conjuring excuses for postponement. Many great ideas and plans remain buried in the minds and hearts of their owners simply because they procrastinate, and they never come to fruition.

I set the wheels in motion. Every day, I donned my iron shoes to obtain permits, running from one office to another. I needed to choose a name for the project, a name I had held in my mind for many years; back to the days when I would visit Astara, right at the spot where I intended to build the hotel. Espinas; a name as renowned as the sturdy Alborz mountains. Espinas is one of the mountain ranges of the Alborz near Astara. Various interpretations exist regarding its name; some say it derives from "Asb" (horse), as the peak resembles a horse's head, while others interpret it as meaning "white peak" or something else entirely. But all interpretations are beautiful. Regardless of its literal meaning, to me, Espinas is a strong and steadfast mountain, blessed with a pleasant climate, towering toward the sky, invincible, a mountain by the sea and the forest; a mountain reaching up to the clear blue sky. It is a mountain rich with ancient and precious artifacts within its heart; a mountain that will symbolize my hotel; one that embodies the very qualities Espinas possesses, enchanting every traveler and tourist who encounters it. What does one want from life except for a cozy corner surrounded by mountains, forests, seas, and skies? A place where, no matter where you look, you will see a manifestation of the Creator's greatness. In its sky, you can soar like a light-footed dove. In the green of its trees, you will dissolve. I obtained the permits and began constructing a beautiful, tranquil hotel for the people. I had a background in construction since childhood; buying, selling, building, working as a laborer; and now I was present at every stage of this hotel's creation.

It was complete. I feel joy and happiness when I see travelers wandering through the hotel and its surroundings, full of laughter and delight. I am touched to see a man holding his elderly mother's hand as they stroll around the hotel, or to watch a little boy playing by the lake with his father, or the many heads peeking out of the hotel windows, perhaps whispering their wishes. God knows what stories lie within each of them, what histories and tales they carry. But I am glad that, nonetheless, staying in this beautiful nature brightens their spirits and temporarily eases their sorrows. May the fresh air, greenery, and unparalleled view of Espinas enrich your existence.

Espinas Astara marked the beginning of a lasting endeavor for me; one that made me acutely aware of all the flaws and deficiencies in this field. Starting something is always difficult. Once you immerse yourself in it, nothing and no one can hinder your progress.

Yet, the place I always dreamed of establishing a hotel was the city where I spent much of my life: Tehran. In a delightful area with good weather, specifically Keshavarz Boulevard near the beautiful Laleh Park. Construction of the hotel in this location also began.

I intended for **Espinas** to be the name of all the hotels I would build. But when others attempt to steal something from your country, when foreign nations seek to distort a part of your homeland in their name, you must rise for your country; even with seemingly small acts like naming a place or building. When the neighboring countries of the Persian Gulf were trying to impose names other than **Persian Gulf** on this ever-enduring Persian Gulf, silence was no longer an option. I decided to name the hotel on Keshavarz Boulevard **Espinas Persian Gulf**. A hotel with a unique architectural style established in 2009, designed to captivate the hearts of every traveler.

Once again, I found myself in Yazd, this time with my family. I will never tire of exploring the old quarters of this city. The sight of the towering windcatchers and the extraordinary architecture of our ancestors never fails to captivate me. A voice in my heart shouted once more: "Do you remember when you were a child, visiting a windcatcher with your family, promising that one day you would create something like it? What happened to that promise? Weren't you supposed to pursue your goals?" This dream tugged at my heart again. I believe that when you feel good, you should listen to the voice within. I feel that God speaks to His servants through the heart. The heart is the language of communication between the Creator and the creation. Every aspiration or dream that enters your heart has the potential to become a reality if you put in the effort.

You shouldn't dwell on your weaknesses; instead, focus on the source of your desires, for every yearning has a destination you must strive for, and you should not lose hope. God doesn't judge you by the greatness of your goals; He looks at your heart. If you find it easy to believe in the realization of your dreams, God will bring them into your life just as easily. Rumi expressed this beautifully:

"If you are not taken there, it is no wonder;
Don't look at your helplessness, but at your yearning,
For this longing is a hostage of God,
And every seeker deserves their sought-after goal.
Strive to increase this longing,
So your heart may rise from the pit of the body.
People say, 'That poor man is such and such,'
But you will say, 'I am alive, O heedless ones!
Though my body may be asleep like others,
Eight heavens have blossomed in my heart.'"

When a goal arises in our minds, it means we have the ability to achieve it. In fact, our desire already exists, and then God plants that yearning in our hearts; we just need to find it through effort and perseverance.

I can no longer postpone today's work for tomorrow. After building two hotels, I had accumulated enough experience. I needed to choose another pleasant area in Tehran for the next hotel, one that offered a view of the entire city. The Saadat Abad region was the most suitable location. In the 1980s, I worked tirelessly to obtain the necessary permits for Espinas Palace, and in 2011, I kicked off the construction of this hotel. As always, I was present at every stage until I reached my ultimate goal, and in 2015, this hotel opened its doors, welcoming numerous guests from across the country and around the world.

I achieved this dream through my patience and hard work. I never waited for someone else to motivate me; I have always been the driving force in my own life. Someone who relies on others to reach their goals will never truly taste success. Even if they do, that success will be fleeting; like a spark or a mirage, lacking permanence. Imagine sitting idly, waiting for someone to come along. What if months pass and no one arrives? What if years of your life are spent in such a hope, and no one shows up? When you finally reach the end of your long journey, what will you have to show for it but regret? Will you find a way back? Never... never... Alas, the water that has flowed cannot return to the river. So, bind your entire life; your goals and dreams; to yourself, and depend on your own efforts, not on external events or people, so that your happiness may be eternal and lasting.

I have always told myself: Ali Asghar, never fear failure; instead, view it as a challenge you must rise above. In fact, great people have experienced far greater failures. Do you think Edison invented electricity on his first try? No, he certainly explored thousands of paths, and each time he made a mistake, he must have thought, "Well done, Edison... I've eliminated one more path that wouldn't lead me to my goal." So, strive harder to cast aside those unhelpful routes and find the one that leads you to light and clarity.

Yes, Ali Asghar Amiri! You must adopt this perspective towards obstacles and challenges. You must not be afraid; you must be courageous. Every second of my life has been driven by a plan and purpose. My friends and classmates would look at me in amazement when they saw me spend five minutes and twenty seconds memorizing a lesson, and I would accomplish it right within that timeframe.

My actions have always been organized; daily, monthly, yearly, short-term, and long-term plans, even hourly or minutely schedules. I remember back in the late '70s, I hung my Alvarex watch on the weaving machine and meticulously planned each minute and second. I often sighed as the red second hand circled the dial while my tasks didn't go according to plan, and it clawed at my being. I always tried to stay a minute or even a few seconds ahead of my schedule to maintain my peace of mind. This approach gave me a higher spirit and fueled my determination to keep moving forward.

I consistently designed very tight schedules for myself, and my productivity was perhaps three to four times greater than that of my colleagues. There was a time when I didn't see the sun in my own home for nearly two years. I felt extremely fatigued, and perhaps doubts about all my efforts crept into my mind. However, at that moment, a technical worker at the weaving factory, seeing my exhaustion, told me, "Asghar, don't feel tired! You are a successful person." His words recharged my spirit, like jump-starting a battery, and I resumed my work with renewed strength.

After the completion of the Espinas Saadat Abad Hotel, I kept my eyes wide open and my ears tuned to catch any flaws or criticisms. Customer satisfaction was incredibly important to me. After all, what value or prestige does a hotel hold without the guests and travelers who come to stay? Sometimes, I would approach the hotel staff, security guards, and valets, engaging them in conversation, hoping to hear insights that could help rectify any shortcomings. I thought that perhaps one of our guests, possessing great wisdom, had shared an idea with them that could enhance our reputation for customer service and attract even more visitors.

It is precisely this sensitivity and the unique architectural style of this hotel that draws travelers from all over the world. Once, the Chinese Minister of Tourism remarked during a meeting with his counterpart in our country that Espinas Saadat Abad Hotel was the only hotel destination for Chinese tourists.

Perhaps it was Cristiano Ronaldo's visit to Iran that introduced more people in my country to this hotel. When fans of this greatest football player surrounded the hotel to catch a glimpse of him, I wished I could welcome each one of them with the utmost respect, rolling out a red carpet beneath their feet. Alas, how I wished the circumstances had allowed for that!

Sometimes, you need to change certain things in your life to see your dreams and goals come to fruition. If you continue down the same path you've walked for years without achieving results, don't expect change in your life; that expectation is misplaced. Often, we harbor subconscious beliefs that subtly shape our feelings and behaviors. I call this belief, which can be either positive or negative. If it's positive, how fortunate is the person who holds that belief, as their mind guides them to their goals with minimal physical effort. However, if it's a false belief, it can destroy a person and darken their days. The subconscious can become combative, steering them away from their dreams and aspirations without their awareness. Unfortunately, most people are unaware of this immense power of their minds and make no effort to change their beliefs, yet they wonder why, despite all their efforts, their lives remain as they were ten years ago.

Yes, if you want your life to be as you desire, you must endure the pain of transformation. Change is a rebirth. A new self will emerge from you. Just as a mother endures the pain of childbirth, you too must endure the discomfort of your own rebirth to create a new life.

One common misconception is that people and external circumstances can hinder you from achieving your goals. If someone believes this, they will never reach great heights. There will always be people and events that try to obstruct your path. Thus, you must replace that belief with another: that everyone has control over their lives, no matter how great the external obstacles may be. Yes, change can be painful.

After completing the Espinas Saadat Abad Hotel, I decided to open another hotel in the pleasant region of Velanjak. However, for many years, I struggled to obtain the necessary permits, facing obstacles from some parties, while only a few supported me with love and hope. But I was not the kind of person to let external circumstances deter me from pursuing my goals; I held myself responsible for everything happening around me.

My mother would recite the Masnavi for me, saying, "Look how beautifully Rumi speaks to us: Every person and everything in the world has its own nature. The moon gives light and continues on its path, while a dog barks, vinegar has its own flavor, and a raven cannot impose its cawing on a nightingale. You, like the moon, should revolve in your own orbit and pursue your path to success; no barking can hinder your shine. With your actions and words, spread sweetness everywhere, for sour-faced vinegar types cannot take this quality from you or affect you from the outside." This advice has always resonated with me, and I kept the poem my mother often recited before my eyes:

"The moon casts light, and the dog barks;

Each person pursues their own creation.

Every person has a duty set by fate,

In accordance with their essence in trials."

Despite all the obstacles, I moved forward with determination and hope toward achieving this goal until, after several years, I finally obtained the permit. I have always progressed along a path of great ideas and thoughts. In addition to physical work, the mind must always be active, nurturing positive and good thoughts. Such a mindset is always wealthy, even if its bank account is empty because this mindset will ultimately lead to abundance and wealth.

On the other hand, a person who takes no action to energize their mind, even if they inherit great wealth by chance, possesses a poor and impoverished mentality. If we look around, we often find that such individuals lose their windfall over time due to their ignorance, spending it on trivial matters. In truth, they are not on the path to wealth and success; they stand in stark contrast to those who are on the straight path of abundance.

Moreover, the law of this world is such that you receive back whatever you give. If you want wealth, you must be generous. If you seek love and affection from others, you must show kindness yourself. If you desire smiles, you must be the one to initiate them. If you do not see love from anyone, look within yourself and seek it there. Perhaps you have not loved yourself and others as you should. Seek love first within yourself.

Whenever a young person sees me, they often express their fear of the difficulties they might face in achieving their goals. They ask me to share the struggles and obstacles I've overcome on my challenging journey. I have faced countless hardships and bitterness to reach my current position. I have endured many trials, moving mountains that stood in my way, yet I never gave up, never backed down, and never relinquished my dreams and aspirations.

In my belief, without hardship, a person cannot appreciate the moments of their life. Without problems and obstacles, happiness and success cannot reveal their true sweetness. The world is fundamentally built on the interplay of good and bad. Without adversity, the virtues we cherish do not shine as they should. Just as the sting of a bee makes the sweetness of honey worthwhile, until you feel the sharpness of a thorn, you will not truly appreciate the beauty of a flower. The foundation of the world is built on struggle, a blend of good and evil; without this balance, the world would not exist.

As Rumi eloquently put it: "This world is a battle; when you look closely,
Particle's clash like faith with disbelief.
One particle moves left, another right,
You see their conflict in the stillness of night."

According to Rumi, the world is founded on the peace and conflict that exist between opposites. Just as the spinning wheel of fate sways, how can human beings, its children, escape this ebb and flow? In times of hardship, I often hear the whispered words of this tender-hearted poet echoing in my mind: "The spinning wheel, ever searching,
Its state mirrors that of its children.
At times low, at times mid, at times high,
In it, a multitude of fortunes and misfortunes fly.
Since all entities experience suffering and pain,
How can a part of them remain unscathed?"

Indeed, I have faced difficulties and endured hardships, but I have always fought with a smile on my lips, striving until my last breath. Now that I have overcome these obstacles, I find little desire to speak of them, for my perspective has always been to see the beauty in life. I never focus on bitterness and hardships, even when they surround me. With all the beauty enveloping me, why should I fixate on the undesirable and the limitations? Instead, we should focus on beauty and goodness to attract more of it into our lives.

This principle, if embraced moment by moment, ensures that one never falters or fails, regardless of the circumstances. The fundamental truth lies within a person's thoughts and mindset, not in the external events surrounding them. Whatever you nurture in your mind, you will see reflected in the world outside. For many years, I have held on to Rumi's words, which have become a constant companion in my heart: "We do not gaze outward at the appearance;

We look within to understand our true state."

The reason I refrain from discussing my hardships, in addition to focusing on the beauty and blessings in my life, is that I worry a young person just embarking on their journey might feel disheartened upon hearing about the challenges I faced. I wouldn't want them to think, "Can anyone really endure such difficulty? Is it possible to wear iron shoes every moment without tiring? Can one persist despite constant setbacks?"

Perhaps everyone can bear a different measure of hardship. The struggles I faced may seem like a towering mountain to one person and merely a small hill to another. I prefer that each individual measures their capacity against their own challenges. Let the novice take pride in overcoming the obstacles that feel monumental to them; hardships that, if I were to speak of them, might seem as light as a feather in comparison to what I have endured. Let them not compare their strength to mine and become disheartened. Instead, let each person build their castle of dreams with a peaceful heart.

Advice from an Entrepreneur

Ali Asghar Amiri is the kind of person whose absence leaves a significant void. He is big-hearted, lovable, experienced, and truly one of a kind. He says, "I want to pass on my wisdom to the younger generation so they can achieve greatness as well. I take pride in those who strive for our country." Listen closely to the values that transform you into a remarkable person like Ali Asghar Amiri.

Write Down Your Tasks and Priorities

I've always had a habit that might prove beneficial for you. Since my teenage years, I developed the practice of mentally reviewing all my plans and tasks. This habit formed when, as some would say today, I was a working child. At the age of 12 or 13, I started working day and night. Even at that young age, I considered everything I needed to accomplish within a day. I knew that my work would provide for my living expenses, which made me think about my future success and progress. Sometimes I wondered why I shouldn't push harder since the work I was doing supported my life. Yet, when I thought about my future achievements, my perspective shifted. It motivated me to work even harder. My advice to the younger generation is to increase their efforts and think about continuous, day-and-night work. Write down your plans and goals. Anything that isn't written down remains a mere thought, a timeless dream. But once you put it on paper, you have the opportunity to revise it as many times as necessary. Writing makes your work feel more serious.

Creating a Significant Difference

When you document your plans and goals, it can create a significant impact in your life. It will greatly enhance your productivity and efficiency. Since my youth, I've been engaged in contract work, calculating how much I should charge for each piece of clothing. There were times I felt like the unluckiest person alive because I worked for an employer who wasn't fair. He wouldn't pay us our full wages, and there was no refrigerator in the workshop for us to use. We didn't even have air conditioning; he would just say, "If you're too hot, open a window for fresh air." The only heater was a small wall heater, installed to warm the machines, not us. When we told him we were cold, he'd respond, "Then just work to warm up." Despite this situation, I never made excuses. Many of my colleagues left, which often resulted in them being unemployed for two or three months until they found their next job. I thought differently: if I left and had to wait three months for the next job, I'd be two months behind if the employer paid a month's wage after two months. I had a plan that helped me navigate my work effectively. That's why I worked diligently to overcome the challenges.

Don't Procrastinate

To our young people, I say that if you have a plan and are working hard, it's natural for your income to grow. However, once your income increases, don't raise your expenses. In personal development, it's often said to tackle the tough tasks first so you can later move on to easier ones. I made it a habit to do the difficult tasks quickly to progress to the simpler ones. I had trained myself not to procrastinate, adhering to my schedule strictly. I worked with a sense of urgency, paying attention to every second. I was extremely punctual, completing my tasks on time without delay. I knew that if I postponed my work, not only would my costs remain unchanged, but I would also have to dip into my savings or cover my current expenses, resulting in a cycle of losses. Therefore, I worked intensely. After three years of hard work, I was finally able to purchase a weaving machine and start my own business.

Don't Settle for the Status Quo

If you have worked hard and saved some money, and your life is going well, don't be satisfied with just that. You deserve to progress further and execute your plans with diligence. If you constantly strive to maintain your current status, you will eventually fade away. Always make it a habit to review your plans and work standards regularly. If you don't have clear standards and don't revisit them frequently, time will slip away quickly. Time is like a fast-moving train, and unless we catch up with it, we will miss opportunities. You should position yourself among those who make an impact in this world. Never waste time. Your worth will stem from your efforts. You've likely heard that time is gold, but once you become accustomed to hard work, your value will surpass gold. You will find that your time becomes far more valuable than any material wealth.

Maintain a Positive Edge in Thinking

To ensure our work progresses well, we must work with a sense of urgency regarding minutes and seconds. We need to prioritize our tasks and goals. This prioritization should be woven into our daily rhythms so we can positively impact our productivity and improve our market standing. We must plan in a way that allows us to gain positive momentum, not negative. Negative momentum means competing with others through sabotage, which is neither right nor fair. Some people resort to any means necessary to gain visibility, but that is not the way. You must create a positive distinction to be noticed. I suggest achieving this distinction by helping others genuinely, without any pretense. When you help, it should come from the heart, not just for show.

I used to start my work early in the morning and continue until late into the night. Sometimes, I worked so hard that I was relieved when five hours had passed, allowing me to rest. I don't recommend working this intensely all the time; I sometimes struggle to forgive myself for how hard I push. You might wonder how far you should go with this hard work. It should continue until you reach a point of success, where your work becomes systematic and flows smoothly, and you're able to find a balance in life, combining work, leisure, and personal time. Once you design this new plan, it's essential to follow through. My motto is: "Follow through, follow through, follow through." Only by pursuing your goals will you reach your destination. If you want your life to take shape quickly, you must be more organized and quicker than others. The train of progress is moving rapidly, and to catch it, you need to get ahead of the others and ensure your plans are coherent.

Remember, all your plans need to be documented so you can refine and execute them. If your plans are merely in your head, they remain a dream; an image without time or feasibility. Every project and aspect of your life requires a plan. Once you complete one project, promptly draft a new plan for the next. Don't waste your days; execute your plans and gather feedback. One prominent Western entrepreneur once said, "In my office, instead of trophies and awards, I only have blueprints and plans," leaving visitors astonished. This is the path to progress.

Don't Procrastinate on Difficult Tasks

Be aware that difficult and challenging tasks must be accomplished regardless. Putting them off will ultimately harm us. We need to start sooner rather than later. If you want to strengthen the foundation of your life, you should begin this work from a young age. In youth, you have energy, capability, and willpower. The longer you delay this work, the more your energy, determination, and capability will wane, making these tasks more difficult for you. Don't think to yourself, "I won't do it now; I'll see how it goes." It won't turn out well; rather, your conditions, situation, and willpower will become tougher, and you won't be able to handle tasks as easily as you did in the past. As one well-known entrepreneurship and management educator says, the tasks you procrastinate on will not be completed in the future; they will be lost forever.

Avoid Negative Language Surrounding Work

My next point is about the rhetoric surrounding work that is often used in negative terms, especially regarding child labor. We should discard this destructive language. If you want to become a successful entrepreneur and businessperson, you need to start hard, diligent work as soon as possible. Completing tasks, even if they lead to failure, is still better than not doing them at all. Ultimately, these experiences will be invaluable for you. With such valuable experiences, you can move your plans forward. You must decide to enter the workforce, work hard, and advance your plans.

Don't Waste Time Strengthening Your Capabilities

Pursuit, perseverance, and grand thoughts are the precursors to your success and work. When you have big ideas, you can take action in any endeavor. You must significantly enhance your abilities. It's beneficial to enter these fields in your teenage years and develop your capabilities so that in the future, these experiences will benefit you. You should not waste any time in strengthening your skills. As I mentioned, you must overcome the habit of procrastination. Do not let tasks fall behind. You should advance and complete tasks in the shortest time possible to achieve success.

Work Hard Day and Night

This truth may not be pleasing to many young people who want to achieve everything quickly. However, the bitter reality is that without putting in tireless effort and incorporating a mindset of hard work into your activities, your capabilities and thinking will not strengthen, and you won't make any progress. Success requires sweat, sleepless nights, and relentless hard work; no one reaches it without these elements. If you progress with love, honesty, and purity, you can generate and create wealth; both material and spiritual. Remember that you must approach the creation of wealth in a systematic and step-by-step manner. Otherwise, your wealth may come by chance and can easily be lost. But if your mind reaches success systematically and step by step, even if you face failure, you can attempt to achieve success again. These are very important points to keep in mind.

Balance Work, Life, and Leisure

Another point is to learn when to enjoy, when to work, when to engage in conversation with those around you, and when to relish life. Remember that life is the path we are on, and we should not search for an extraordinary thing called life. Our work and efforts are part of life, especially when done with love and enjoyment. Working with joy does not tire us; on the contrary, it elevates us. Those who become professionals are the ones who passionately engage with their work, making good work a part of their lives. Let's remember to enjoy this train called life we are on. We shouldn't obsess over reaching the destination. Can you guarantee that the destination will be as beautiful as the journey we are taking? Don't think of the hard work you are doing as a type of suffering. Many would love to be in your place and work in this way. Simply working with love and serving others is truly sufficient for enjoying life. Even if your job is to produce disposable cups and dishes, you should think, "I am providing clean dishes for someone to enjoy their life, and that is a form of service; what could be better than this?"

Create Lasting Work

Work has energy; it speaks to you. The products you create and the services you provide communicate with you. Therefore, strive to perform your work with love, interest, and quality. In this way, you infuse your spirit and heart into your work, making it enduring. Others will notice the signals of love and interest emanating from this work, and they will be drawn to it. What could be better than this?

Cultivate a Wealthy Mindset

I see young people who constantly complain about their family situation, their parents, their city, and their life. They use their difficult circumstances as an excuse for their lack of success. This is not right. You must strive for wealth, achievement, and success through your own efforts. Your mindset should be wealthy, not poor. One day, a poor person found a bundle of money in front of a bank and returned it to the bank. The bundle belonged to one of the customers and contained a significant amount of money. Some would have thought, "Why should I return it? I'll keep it for myself." But he did the right thing because he had a wealthy mindset. The bank manager was so impressed by his action that he hired him to manage the bank's wealthy clients because he demonstrated that he had a healthy and sound mindset. People should produce authenticity with their healthy behaviors. Young people should plan and work in such a way that they can change their circumstances.

Motivation and Positive Thinking

Your thoughts can create wealth for you. You must learn to cultivate your thoughts with planning, effort, and motivation. If you cannot create motivation, you will not be able to create wealth. If you work well, you can reach a point where, even with limited resources, you can create something for yourself. This creation does not necessarily have to be artistic; it can be a product, a service, or anything else in life. You must learn to think positively to create positive events around you. If your thoughts are negative, you will only generate negative outcomes. Pay attention to these matters.

Analysis of the Success Factors of the Founder of Espinas Hotel Chain

Perhaps the main discussion on the principles of success and personal development becomes much clearer when illustrated with an example from Brian Tracy. Brian Tracy is one of the most respected names in the field of personal development. However, he once worked as a manual laborer, doing physical tasks. He traveled on ships to various countries to move goods. When he could no longer continue this work, he decided to pursue a career in sales. He joined a company and started working. But no matter how hard he tried, he found little success. Then one day, he asked himself:

- **What do successful salespeople at my company do differently?**

This question led him to approach them and ask for their insights. Generously, they shared their secrets with him. Brian implemented these strategies and noticed a significant impact. The more he applied their techniques, the better his results became. He then thought about seeking advice from successful salespeople at other companies as well. By discovering and applying their secrets, he achieved even better results. He turned to books to uncover more secrets, leading to yet more improvements in his performance. He attended workshops and conferences, and again saw better outcomes. He consulted with advisors and gathered information, which further enhanced his situation.

His performance in the company improved so dramatically that he first became the sales manager and then the company's director. However, during his tenure as a manager, he encountered challenges and lost some of his top salespeople. Why did this happen? He was one of the top salespeople himself, so why was he facing these difficulties? Brian reflected on his early days in the company and pondered what good managers do that he wasn't doing. He reached out to successful managers to uncover their strategies. By implementing these, he noticed his results improving again. He realized that management was vastly different from being a salesperson. He sought knowledge from various consultants, books, workshops, and conferences, continuously learning and applying new insights, which led to further improvements. Eventually, he became a highly paid manager, and ultimately, a rival company hired him at three times his previous salary. When he left his company, he realized that no one in the company's history had been paid as much as he was. In his books, he often expresses his amazement at the simplicity and power of success principles; all it takes is to observe what successful people do and repeat those actions more vigorously. In fact, the entire literature of personal development and success principles began with this question:

Why are some people more successful than others? What can we do to achieve greater success?

Reflecting on such questions helps one gradually gain knowledge and experience in their field and life, ultimately contributing to the literature of personal development. At the core of this knowledge is the belief that individuals can change their circumstances. For a long time, humanity didn't believe in the power to change personal or even social conditions. Any change that did occur was often the result of struggles among forces and powers, rather than a clear individual or collective idea. However, in the last two or three centuries, humanity has increasingly armed itself with knowledge, which has granted the power to influence and change their surroundings and nature. Gradually, people began to realize that many of the things they attributed to fate or chance were not as they perceived. They learned to gain control over their environments, applying this approach to their personal lives as well, leading to positive outcomes. The realization that they could change their conditions and have the power to shape their circumstances in their favor fueled their enthusiasm, generating the energy of success that continued to grow.

One of the most significant aspects of success literature is learning from the achievements of others and how they overcame challenges. When we see how others have tackled their problems and advanced towards their desired conditions, we are inspired to replicate those experiences. We think to ourselves, "They are just like us." The biographies of individuals like Ali Asghar Amiri, the founder of luxury and prestigious hotels, exemplify this.

Analysis of the Success Factors of
the Founder of Espinas Hotel Chain

Chapter One

Everyone Has Their Own Path to Success

One of the interesting points raised by Mr. Amiri is the importance of sharing experiences. He notes that he has gone through strange memories and difficult days but sees no necessity to share them all with others. But why? What is the reason behind this caution in sharing memories and the risks of entrepreneurial life? Perhaps the answer to this question is one of the great secrets of success; one that many in this field may overlook. The truth is that success is a unique and individual experience for everyone. Just as each person's goals are specific to them, so too are their successes. While everyone can benefit from the experiences of others, it doesn't mean that everything will unfold exactly the same way for everyone. But what does all this mean? Let's elaborate.

Mohammad Reza Ale Yasin, in the captivating book "How the Wealthy Think," written by Charles Albrecht Poissant and translated by him, highlights some intriguing points. His discussion revolves around examining the lives and perspectives of some of the most successful and wealthiest individuals. In one chapter, he emphasizes that everyone has their own specific plan for work and life. For example, while many advise early rising as a key to success, he recounts the story of a wealthy individual who didn't always arrive at work on time and would even show up at the office late at night to manage operations, sometimes even making bizarre decisions, like summoning all his managers in the middle of the night and firing those sitting on his right! While we do not endorse such actions, the point is that everyone can have their own unique rules for success, and there is no obligation for everyone to follow a single approach.

Everything Begins with Self-Discovery

In fact, we must emphasize that everything starts with self-discovery. Paris Pritchett, in his engaging book "The Readable Optimism," makes interesting references to the unique abilities of humans. According to him, these special abilities are tasks that individuals can perform effortlessly, learn quickly, and find so easy that they don't even see them as advantages. They assume everyone can do these tasks just as easily. The point he raises is that each person can have their own special abilities according to their unique talents. Indeed, these unique abilities can differ significantly from one individual to another, and as we all know, these very abilities are what lead to people's successes and wealth. Therefore, it is not possible to prepare a uniform list for everyone to follow in their lives. Of course, there is no doubt that we can learn from successful individuals. However, the distinction between learning from experiences and the necessity to imitate their actions is crucial. When you seek to learn from others' experiences, you are discussing the essence of success; whereas when you focus on the behaviors of others, it's as if you are only paying attention to the form.

It is natural for all of us to need a bathroom, kitchen, living room, and bedroom at home; no one doubts that. But the notion that all these should conform to a single model is unacceptable and fundamentally undermines the diversity of human nature.

Subtle Nuances of Success

We have raised all these points to highlight the necessity of exercising utmost caution when revisiting the experiences of successful individuals. In fact, each person should study and analyze themselves based on their abilities, engaging in a healthy competition with themselves. In this context, it is worth revisiting insights from Dr. Mostafa Malekian, an Iranian intellectual, who explains the overall situation quite well. In one of his lectures to students, he discussed the concepts of satisfaction and success, categorizing people according to these two or a combination of both. In parts of his fascinating lecture, he states:

"I have been asked to discuss competing with oneself and comparing oneself to past selves; a discussion I have addressed before, but I'm unsure if it has been published anywhere. In a general psychological categorization, we humans can be divided into two groups: those who are oriented towards success and those who are oriented towards satisfaction. This is a broad classification.

One group consists of those who are success-oriented (success). These individuals exhibit four key characteristics:

1. Comparison and Competition: In their normal states of awareness, like the one we are in now, they are always mentally and conceptually comparing themselves to others. They see themselves in competition with others. Therefore, whenever they engage in contemplation and thought, they are aware of their standings relative to others; whether they feel they are lagging behind or ahead, and how others are positioned in comparison.

2. Field of Competition: The second characteristic pertains to what they consider the field or direction of competition or comparison. They typically assess themselves against seven social desirables: 1. Wealth; 2. Power (specifically political power); 3. Social status; 4. Fame; 5. Reputation; 6. Popularity; 7. Academic or scholarly knowledge, which they obtain through formal education and publications. For someone caught up in these comparisons and competitions, their situation can worsen progressively. A person might focus solely on one domain, such as academic knowledge or wealth, comparing themselves only in that area. But when they attempt to simultaneously compare in wealth, power, knowledge, and social status, their challenges multiply significantly.

3. Feelings of Success and Failure: The third characteristic is that whenever they see themselves ahead in comparisons, they feel victorious, and when they perceive themselves behind, they feel defeated. They do not regard the outcome of these comparisons; whether a defeat or a victory; as mere experiences. Instead, they correlate their feelings of success and failure directly with these comparisons. In other words, it seems their philosophy of life revolves around whom to surpass and whom not to lag behind, equating advancement with victory and regression with defeat. Consequently, their feelings of success or failure are intrinsically tied to these perceptions.

4. Social Identity: The fourth characteristic of this group is that their identity is entirely social. They lack individual identity. Why? Because their yardstick is success and failure, which they perceive only within the context of social life. Thus, if you were to ask them to define themselves, their definition would revolve around being ahead or behind others. Their identity is perpetually social. They cannot define themselves through their individuality because their essence is fundamentally linked to their victories and defeats in relation to their fellow citizens, friends, and family members. This identity is fundamentally collective and social; they lack an individual identity. They could possess individual traits but have overlooked them from their perspective. They define themselves solely in comparison with others, and their identification is only possible within the realm of social life.

In his continued speech, Dr. Malekian points out that these individuals lead uninteresting lives, both internally and externally, as they always feel they are falling behind others. They often have incorrect benchmarks for comparison, leading to a persistent state of depression. Positions, families, times, and circumstances are entirely different from one another. The energy of a 50-year-old is vastly different from that of a 20-year-old. How can these two be at the same starting line? Therefore, such comparisons are fundamentally flawed. Because they are flawed, they become the breeding ground for sadness, depression, lethargy, fatigue, and feelings of inadequacy. They believe they are always lagging behind others, and anyone in such a position will surely suffer from depression and fatigue.

Dr. Malekian wisely highlights that individual differ significantly in their physical, mental, psychological, moral, and social characteristics; thus, it is impossible to compare everyone in the same way. He then refers to those engaged in seeking life satisfaction, noting that their most important trait is competing with themselves; not in social aspects, but in psychological areas such as hope, happiness, and contentment, which is a wealth without an end.

These were the key points we needed to address regarding Ali

Asghar Amiri's discussions. While it is true that all successful individuals have outstanding experiences, their insights may not necessarily apply to everyone. The level of effort and perseverance exhibited by these individuals might far exceed the average or even good levels found among most people. One day, Dr. Fattahi, the founder of Emersun, was asked about the saying, "You must work like Benz, based on the slogan 'Be the best or be nothing.'" He explained that this slogan fits a company in that situation, but it does not suit us as humans. We are individuals striving for our own form of perfection at a normal level, and there will be times when we may not be the best; sometimes, we need to be just good or even experience failure. Being average or below average in our human journey is perfectly natural and evident, and we must learn from it.

Here, we need to understand that the teachings of success from anyone should be carefully examined before being shared with others. In fact, we should consider success as a contextual matter; each person must define and explain their own success based on their circumstances, abilities, social class, education, and intelligence. Otherwise, if we simply adopt others' teachings, we risk becoming more depressed and disheartened. This is because, by looking to others, we constantly strive, and when those efforts yield no results, we feel disheartened and attempt to combat that depression by trying even harder. This cycle continues until depression reaches a point where it no longer motivates us to strive but merely leaves us immobilized. This is where we begin to appreciate the depth of what Ali Asghar Amiri, the founder of the Espinas Hotels, discusses.

Chapter Two

The Golden Rule of Perseverance

Whenever we delve into entrepreneurship and starting a business, one of the most obvious traits that everyone should possess; and one we must discuss extensively; is perseverance. Perseverance means that we do not tire of our work; we maintain spiritual, mental, and physical resilience, and we do not give up until we reach our goals. The differences among people in this domain can often be evaluated based on their perseverance scores, which is why they can often achieve different positions and successes. In reality, possessing this trait is so crucial that it suffices; though we always recommend that one should consider other aspects of success and personal and economic development as well. But how can such a trait alone lead to significant differences?

The Progress Theory

Brian Tracy presents this concept well in one of his books. He refers to a principle known as the Progress Theory. He cites an experiment in which scientists placed several lab mice in a convoluted maze. Interestingly, the mice that put forth the most effort were the ones that managed to discover the exit designed within the maze. In contrast, those that assumed they could not succeed from the outset ended up trapped and going nowhere. The persistent mice tried various paths, returned when necessary, and eventually found the final exit. This experiment was also replicated with flies or bees trapped in a container, where the exit was at the top. Most gave up at the very beginning, while those who worked hard made enough attempts that they eventually found the way out.

This demonstrates that simply being willing to try can lead to progress. You may have noticed many ordinary people who lack a clear idea or vision yet have achieved success. They wake up in the morning and start working, repeating this daily routine. Ultimately, their trial and error pay off, leading them to victory. Of course, the final recommendation is to work smart; however, in the absence of intelligent activity, just having perseverance can still lead you to success. As the saying goes, perseverance and effort never betray us; they will always be good friends. This is why we assert that sheer effort and determination can open doors for us and that they do lead somewhere meaningful.

A Principle from Anthony Robbins

If you're still not convinced about this matter, let me share one of the best and most straightforward success formulas mentioned by Anthony Robbins in his books. This formula consists of four steps. To achieve any success you desire, you must enter the first stage and then continue step by step. The formula is as follows:

First, know what you want.

Take action to achieve it.

Gather feedback from the results to see if they bring you closer to your goal or take you further away.

After making necessary adjustments, return to the second step.

It's a simple and straightforward formula. The crucial point here is that you have four stages, half of which focus on taking action. At the beginning, you need to clarify your direction. As Zig Ziglar puts it, in this journey, direction is more important than intensity, and a compass is more important than a clock. Once you understand your direction and purpose, you should act quickly. You don't need to waste too much time on elaborate planning. Dr. Schwartz, in his engaging book "The Magic of Thinking Big," dedicates a chapter to action. He notes that while planning is good, it should quickly lead to action. He shares an interesting example of a brother and sister who were looking for jobs. The sister began studying how to create a professional resume, a process that took her a week. Meanwhile, her brother quickly contacted job listings and started working on the second dayjus;t that simply.

Brian Tracy points out that when you cultivate the habit of taking action, you will acquire all the necessary information along the way, through the feedback you receive; just as Anthony Robbins suggests. This is why many uneducated and less specialized individuals who have a habit of trying and taking action achieve greater success than those who are educated and qualified. They take action, and through the feedback they receive, they navigate the process of trial and error and move forward.

Experience: More Important than Knowledge

In the engaging book about the teachings of Gurdjieff, we observe a student who leaves his life in the heart of Europe to seek out the Gurdjieff masters; individuals who have played a significant role in his education. In this journey, he discovers his own path and realizes that he must learn the principles that transformed his teacher into Gurdjieff, rather than merely searching for his teacher's teachers. At one point, an intriguing dialogue occurs between him and one of Gurdjieff's masters:

"I asked Sheikh Abdollah Shatter: If I don't ask questions, how will I learn? Sheikh replied: Pay attention to your question; learning and questioning are two different things. You learn through action, not by asking questions. The issue isn't why you should read a specific book or when and where to read it; rather, you should read the book to experience its contents and apply them. You feel compelled to ask questions, and you justify that you have the right to do so, thinking you possess enough intellect and insight to understand the answers. You certainly have a higher education and a university degree. But does your 'intellect and insight' help you in the field of handicrafts if you lack skill and experience? Do skin diseases heal faster if you hold a university degree? Can you run faster than a trained yet uneducated runner just because you are wiser? Does your intelligence grant wing to your feet? Education, intellect, and knowledge are only beneficial when you can apply them correctly and in the right context."

The essence of this message is clear: we learn through action and experience, not by questioning and studying. Learning and education can be useful and constructive only when they lead to action and experience; otherwise, they serve no real purpose. Jack Canfield, in his book "Success Principles," emphasizes that the world's greatest rewards are not given to those with the most knowledge, but to those who act on their knowledge.

The Goal: To Remain Hardworking

Let me share a quote from Farzad Habibollah, a football analyst who worked alongside Branko, the coach of Persepolis Football Club. Under Branko, Persepolis achieved numerous honors, including consecutive championships and the runner-up position in Asia. Branko, renowned for his strategic thinking, was even called "the professor" during his time with the Croatian national team when they secured third place in the World Cup. Habibollah mentions:

"The night before the game against Al Rayyan in Tehran, I discussed his football philosophy with Branko after dinner. I asked: 'Isn't one of the most delicate aspects of a coach's job about harmonizing inherently divergent elements? In your football philosophy, both the players' patience during the game and their speed with the ball are essential. How does a coach maintain a relatively calm demeanor in various situations while keeping the team hungry and offensive?' Branko replied: 'I have always tried to remain normal in my life. Striving for normality and normal behavior has been one of my lifelong goals, and what I want to instill in my team is to remain ambitious and hardworking, yet relatively normal.' Two nights before the game against Al Wahda in Tehran, when our win alone is not enough and we need Al Rayyan to draw against Al Hilal in Qatar for Persepolis to advance from the group stage, Branko discusses our inner desire to see our families proud of us after each win. He states, 'It is so enjoyable to win in football and see your family members proud of you. However, this shouldn't be the main goal. The main goal is to remain hardworking. Hard work, if treated merely as a means, can yield temporary success, but it should be the primary goal of the coach and the team to increase the likelihood of repeated success.' A few hours ago, we had our final practice for the first week of the league, while one of the hardest-working men on the team is still our head coach. One day before the league starts, I reflect on the cycle in my mind: 'Victory brings ease. Ease breeds laziness. Laziness leads to disorder. Disorder results in failure.' This cycle is one reason why championships and honors are passed around in top European football. Branko's emphasis on hard work becomes even more significant after reviewing this cycle, as it highlights the need to prevent potential complacency caused by success. Every team that maintains continuity in success has such principles deeply embedded in its work philosophy. Just two months ago, Persepolis finished a fantastic season by winning the league and advancing to the final eight of the Champions League. However, each of us must internally accept that the goal is to remain hardworking at the level of the last season, as if there were no championship at all. The goal transcends victory or the joy of seeing loved ones; the goal is to remain hardworking; something that keeps the team away from self-deception, laziness, disorder, and the certainty of failure."

Why We Need Extraordinary Perseverance

Branko has articulated the main point here: if your goal is hard work, you will achieve greater successes and never feel exhausted. However, if you merely pursue results and use hard work as a means to an end, you will tire quickly and lose the joy in your heart. This is where we note that perseverance, even when it exists solely, can propel you forward. Furthermore, this perseverance should not only meet the ordinary standard; it should sometimes exceed it; pushing beyond our limits and fatigue. The obstacles that arise in this journey demand more energy and strength than usual to overcome. This is why our perseverance must sometimes be extraordinary, enabling us to address these uncommon challenges. Here, insights from Darren Hardy, the author of "The Compound Effect" and an entrepreneur, can be very enlightening. He provides points that demonstrate that there is no such thing as easy success, and one must work hard, dismissing the myths and misleading advertisements surrounding this topic. Darren Hardy begins by discussing momentum or significant results, writing:

"In this chapter, I want to discuss a principle that has brought many extraordinarily successful individuals to this point: the principle of momentum. Here, I intend to delve into Newton's first law: an object at rest remains at rest until an external force act upon it; an object in motion remains in motion unless acted upon by another force. This means that every motion continues in the same direction until an obstacle arises. But how does this relate to success?

Success Through the Lens of Newton's First Law

Have you ever ridden a carousel in your childhood? You know, the ones that spin around in the park? To get these carousels moving, you need to exert a lot of energy and run to set them in motion. Once they start moving, you can step off and let them continue spinning until some external force interrupts that motion. Success operates in a similar manner. To achieve significant momentum, you need to invest a great deal of initial energy and effort. But once you accomplish this, you will continue on your path to success. Just like Newton's first law, you will keep moving forward as long as nothing or no one interferes with your progress. Think of a space rocket; it expends enormous energy and fuel to overcome Earth's gravity. Once it escapes this gravitational pull and leaves Earth's atmosphere, it continues on its trajectory. This is the great secret of successful people; those who seem to grow more successful, happier, wealthier, and more developed every day. They are in motion; according to Newton's first law, an object at rest remains at rest until a force act upon it, and conversely. To achieve this momentum, several stages must be followed:

1. Make new choices that align with your inner values.
2. Turn these choices into behaviors.
3. These behaviors must be repeated to become habitual.
4. Establish routines and processes in your life that lead to this momentum.
5. To achieve the results of the compound effect, you must remain steadfast for an extended period.

The Great Sudden Change

Suddenly, that big change happens! When you stay committed to this process, a sudden and significant shift will occur. Of course, it's not entirely sudden; years of effort, discipline, structure, and energy have gone into it. But that momentum is created all at once. The result? You have created something incredibly important. Think of Michael Phelps, the legendary swimmer. He won eight gold medals at the Beijing Olympics and is currently the most decorated Olympic and world athlete. But how did Phelps reach such heights? His coach devised a training plan for him that he had to adhere to for twelve years. In those twelve years, he only finished his training early once, and that was for just fifteen minutes, to attend a friend's wedding. Imagine that; twelve years and only one fifteen-minute concession! That's why the sudden change occurs, leading him to win all those medals. The same applies to other greats like Steve Jobs and Bill Gates.

Turning Habits into Routines

Let's talk a bit about routines and the power they hold. Many of the things we want to do and many of the goals we have don't yield results simply because we lack the proper mechanisms to execute them. A proper mechanism means having a routine. A routine means doing things automatically, without the need for thought or struggle. It's that simple; you perform tasks without overthinking. Interestingly, the more significant and serious the challenge you face, the more precise and serious the routines you need to adhere to become. Have you ever seen military personnel? Even tying their shoelaces, polishing their shoes, and waking up has a specific order and routine. These routines are both detailed and consistent, which is why military personnel become skilled and experienced within a few months, able to instinctively handle their tasks even in the most challenging circumstances.

Routines Make You Unstoppable

All successful individuals not only have good habits but also have clear routines in their daily lives. That's why they can achieve success easily. I have such routines in my life. From the moment I wake up in the morning, I know exactly what tasks I need to perform without thinking or debating. This includes reflecting on things I'm grateful for, doing stretches while preparing my coffee, etc. Then I spend half an hour on motivational reading, followed by an hour of working on an important project. I continue like this, and my life has a clear routine. You should be the same. You need to follow these routines to reach that big change.

Of course, I understand that this process can be exhausting. You can mix things up in your routines occasionally so it doesn't become overly tedious. Additionally, these routines should evolve into a rhythm. Only then will you get closer to that big shift.

Unusual Persistence and Overexertion

There was a time when I lived in a city in California. Sometimes, to build and train my willpower, I would ride my bike uphill for two or three miles. When you try to cycle uphill, it feels like time stands still, and there's no end in sight. Even cycling champions like Lance Armstrong have experienced this and written about it in their biographies. You reach a point where reality hits hard; you either push forward to discover your strengths or retreat and confront your weaknesses. In these moments, you hit a wall, which we call the walls of limitation. Your ability to either break through or not break through these walls will determine if you'll reach success.

Show Up More Than More

During my time in the real estate business, I encountered many such situations. I would sometimes miss opportunities to visit houses at the right moment, resulting in missed chances. In those moments, I became incredibly frustrated and would turn back, but I never surrendered. I told myself that my competitors and colleagues were also working under similar circumstances. I realized that if I wanted to win, I had to push ahead, disregarding those pains, limitations, and failures.

Lou Holtz, the famous rugby coach, understood this concept well; he believed that doing more than your maximum capacity leads to success. He asked his players to push beyond their limits. Why? Because he knew all players in rugby, across all teams, expend their maximum effort. What matters is uncovering something beyond that maximum effort; something that others don't do, which sets you apart. During one game, even while trailing 42 to 0 in the first half, he managed to lead his team to victory in the second half using this principle.

The Principle that Made Muhammad Ali Victorious

Let me give you another example. There's no debate that Muhammad Ali is one of the greatest boxers in history. In one of his toughest finals, he competed against George Foreman. Even his most serious fans doubted he could defeat Foreman. George Foreman was a boxer who had previously defeated Muhammad Ali in just two rounds. So, hope was low. However, Ali employed a smart strategy to defeat Foreman. What was his strategy?

Ali aimed to push Foreman to his limits. He knew Foreman was powerful but lacked stamina. So, he leaned against the ropes of the ring, protecting his face with his guard while absorbing Foreman's relentless punches. By the eighth round, Ali's strategy worked; Foreman reached the limits of his endurance and could no longer continue. That's when Ali finished the fight in his favor.

Efforts Beyond Adequacy

When we talk about walls of limitations, we are not referring to your weaknesses. In fact, these limitations can be your strengths. This is where, with a bit more energy and effort, you can gain the upper hand. As Jim Rohn says, don't wish for fewer obstacles; wish for yourself to become stronger. The wall of limitation pushes you to achieve greater success, even exponentially.

But how can you multiply results in this area? It's quite simple: exert more effort than your maximum capacity. Imagine you are set to complete a set of twelve exercises. When you reach the twelfth exercise, you've essentially achieved your goal. But how can you push yourself to perform five more repetitions, taking your bicep curls up to seventeen? Because you have exerted yourself beyond your maximum energy, the results you achieve through this surprising process will multiply over time. This is where true progress lies.

Arnold Schwarzenegger is a great example in this regard. He believes that unless you overcome the burning sensation caused by those extra reps, you won't reach your goals. That burning sensation signifies growth; it means you are progressing, as your body struggles to cope with the imposed pressure, compelling it to become stronger. This strengthening manifests as soreness in your muscles. So, you must endure it. By doing so, the results you achieve will multiply several times over. Just like runners who reach a specific distance and experience a burning sensation in their lungs and limbs; going just a little further can lead to significant growth in their abilities. These extra efforts and that one additional lap each day will ultimately turn you into a champion and exponentially increase your results. You must exert more than enough and step ahead of yourself and your previous results.

Surpass Expectations

When we expand this principle, we arrive at the concept of surpassing expectations. Oprah Winfrey is an excellent example in this regard. In everything she undertakes, she goes far beyond and well above expectations. She made headlines at the start of one season of her show; the media constantly talked about her and her program after her performance. She invited eleven people to her show, whose acquaintances had written to her saying they urgently needed cars. She called them to the stage and gifted each of them a car. But the twelfth car was on its way. She distributed boxes among the audience and announced that the key to the twelfth car was hidden in one of these boxes. Excitement reached its peak. But the real excitement came when everyone opened their boxes to find a key inside each one; they all received cars! What could be better than this?

Our World is a World of Ordinary Things

In our world, everyone is looking for the famous, and this signifies being ordinary. From my perspective, famous things are ordinary, and you need to appear extraordinary. Don't think that this little extra requires more effort, cost, and energy; sometimes, it just takes a bit more intelligence and creativity. During my time in the real estate business, I would carry "sold" signs with me to the houses, telling potential sellers that these signs would be beneficial if they hired me to sell their house. This action significantly increased our chances of success. Sometimes, all it takes is a little more intelligence; that's all.

A Real-Life Example

This is the very point that has led individuals like Ali Asghar Amiri to success. He mentions that he comes from a desert region, renowned for its hard-working and appreciative inhabitants who know the value of what they have, having earned everything through hard work. If you observe closely, people from this geography tend to be notably diligent, appreciate their possessions better, and exhibit greater flexibility in dealing with challenges. The desert, drought, and lack of water are obstacles that require a significant degree of adaptability and high tolerance to overcome. All these characteristics are reflected in Mr. Amiri, resulting in the successes we see today.

It's famously said that Yaqub Layth Safar, the founder of the Safavid dynasty, gathered an army around him when he decided to fight against the Arabs and the Abbasid caliph. You probably know that he was from Sistan, from that same arid, desert, drought-ridden area. One day, his soldiers observed Yaqub Layth standing atop a height in his heavy iron armor and helmet, sword in hand, under the scorching sun. Everyone looked at him in astonishment. The sun was beating down harshly, and everyone was becoming restless, but Yaqub stood firm without flinching. Hours passed until the sun began to set, and he finally came down. His soldiers followed his example; they learned from his patience, tolerance, and endurance, transforming these qualities into their own.

The Subtle Beauty of Overexertion

And this quality applies to you as well. You must exert more effort to enjoy the subtle beauty of that additional effort. Let's say you spend thirty minutes a day reading. You can aim for thirty-five minutes a day or even forty. Although this seems easy, it's that little extra that creates the ultimate change. Your commitment to excellence will yield significant dividends in your life. If you read just five more pages daily, it will result in an extra eighteen hundred pages each year! Just imagine the vast library you could create.

And this applies to everything. If you train harder, whether through your exercise or learning, you can reach that level of unexpected results. As I always say, it's in the unexpected moments that you discover incredible opportunities.

You know, many students achieve high grades without significant effort. When others put in tons of effort, some students gain more rewards without even studying or reading. And yet, they find it strange that it becomes a habit for them. This leads to complacency. Those students begin to fall short in the next levels because they never faced challenges during their early days.

But you have to embrace those challenges; without them, you can't push through. Your goal should be to overcome every expectation and remain steadfast in achieving the desired results.

Chapter Three

Clock or Compass?

One interesting aspect of Ali Asghar Amiri's life is his exceptional sense of direction from a young age. He recounts how, during his adolescence, he observed a relative involved in clothing production and noticed that their situation was better than his own. This motivated him to pursue work in that field. As a result, he went to the workplace of this relative but was unable to find them. However, he started working elsewhere and, as he puts it, learned to weave clothes in just a month.

The Condition for Success

This principle is one of the key aspects of personal and economic success. You may have seen many people who work extremely hard and invest countless hours in their jobs but still fail to achieve their goals. It's likely they wonder why they aren't getting anywhere. A significant reason for this could be that they are on the wrong path. Naturally, someone who wishes to attain great wealth cannot pursue this through a regular employee salary. They must create a business, establish a factory, or consider investing; often referred to as the sacred grail of wealth accumulation. In essence, every goal you set creates its own path and channel. For example, the specific path to gaining strength involves weight training, proper nutrition, and body care; undoubtedly, if you stray down the path of an unhealthy lifestyle and fast food, you won't reach your destination. Every path and process define where you will end up. This is why we say that direction can be even more crucial than effort. If you are heading in the wrong direction, the more you strive, the more you will actually fall behind. However, if you are on the right path, even your ordinary efforts, provided they are consistent, will lead you to the right destination; albeit perhaps taking more time.

What Matters More Than Effort

Zig Ziglar famously stated that, in the journey to success, the compass is more important than the clock. The clock symbolizes the effort and time you invest in working hard, while the compass indicates the direction you should take. If you find yourself lost in a forest, it is your compass and sense of direction that will save you, not excessive effort. Similarly, in the forest of poverty and personal and economic problems, if you do not know the right direction, no amount of hard work will yield results. This is why we emphasize that children should take personality tests and aptitude assessments from an early age to understand their traits and the paths they should pursue. Being on the right path accounts for nearly eighty percent of success. If you are on this path, working harder will yield multiple successes and greater achievements. This is where we talk about smart hard work; effort based on a correct direction, utilizing the right tools, and guided by the right mindset; meaning you know exactly what actions need to be taken, how they should be done, and in which direction.

The Entrepreneur Who Discovered Direction Early

From his teenage years, Ali Asghar Amiri was equipped with the tools of comparison and keen observation. He easily recognized which of his relatives was engaged in what work and who had a better situation. Thus, in his youthful days, he realized that he needed to pursue this path and actively set himself on it. This correct sense of direction, coupled with his intrinsic hard work, which he carried from his life in the desert, enabled him to achieve the results you see today.

If you remember, we mentioned Anthony Robbins' simple and definitive formula for success, which includes four steps:

1. Know exactly what you want.
2. Take actions that lead to that goal.

3. Seek feedback on whether your actions are yielding the intended results.
4. If your actions aren't aligning with your goal, change your approach and try again.

Keep in mind that self-awareness is crucial on this path. It's essential to know where you want to end up. In reality, seeking feedback means checking whether your actions are steering you in the desired direction. If they aren't, there's no need to continue; you must quickly correct your course.

Chapter Conclusion

Remaining Insights

The Secret of a Thriving Market

One fascinating point that Mr. Amiri raises is that when he started working in the clothing industry, he never felt that the market was sluggish; he always believed in its vibrancy. But why is this? Why do others not experience the same? It all comes down to perspective and outlook. One of the prominent Iranian entrepreneurs shared that for him and his team, success in work was paramount. They focused on performing their tasks well and then sought financial returns. This didn't mean they worked aimlessly; their top priority was proving their efficiency and providing a defensible output before claiming financial rewards. In contrast, most people primarily pursue financial gains first.

Amiri mentions that when he was involved in clothing production, he aimed to maintain low profit margins and, as he puts it, be fair. This approach helped him attract numerous customers. He worked diligently to maintain high production volumes, allowing the overall production costs to be distributed across this bulk production, leading to greater profits. This strategy enabled him to advance gradually and achieve more success. This method allows individuals to maintain a good status even with small profits, and even during downturns, they can keep progressing.

In reality, if we strive to put aside greed and proceed steadily, we will only need the law of compound effect and consistency to achieve remarkable successes. Unfortunately, many young people today are so greedy regarding work and the market that they end up missing many initial opportunities. Did all the athletes and artists who are at the peak today start out at the top? Certainly not. They began their journeys, even if their beginnings weren't impressive. However, their ultimate goal was to find value in such humble beginnings.

The Unyielding Mindset

Feeling tired in the realm of entrepreneurship and economic development is unacceptable, as Ali Asghar Amiri points out. He states that everything is like a race; you can't simply declare you're tired and give up midway. Anyone who feels fatigued along the way will surely face failure, whether as a worker, manager, or investor. Here, the concept of endurance has both a mental and a physical aspect. Even the physical aspect is nourished by the mental one. Mentally, you must be foreign to the notion of surrender, and until you reach your goal, you cannot allow yourself to feel exhausted. In essence, you have no right to feel tired. As a manager, entrepreneur, or business creator, you should be an energy producer around you, not an energy consumer. When you are an energy producer, you become a support for others, enabling them to perform at their best. When you hold such a mindset, your body will also cooperate with you and will not feel tired. This mentality will generate energy and free you from stress and anxiety. From this perspective, entrepreneurship and personal development resemble rock climbing; you have no right to tire out, and everything will only conclude once you reach the finish line. Otherwise, in the middle of the earth and sky, your downfall and failure will be inevitable.

When Nothing Feels Heavy

There's a Japanese proverb that states, "He who carries no burden achieves many successes." This saying can have two dimensions: a mental and a physical one. Physically, it means no task should feel heavy for you, and you shouldn't think, "Oh my God, who will do all this work?" Instead, you should dive into tasks with speed and not let them intimidate you. On the other hand, the more critical aspect of this proverb lies in the mental realm; nothing should feel heavy for you mentally. But what does this mean?

Some individuals resist performing certain tasks or holding certain positions in their minds. They might feel that such tasks are beneath their dignity or that, given their education and qualifications, they shouldn't have to do them. However, it is the work itself that holds importance, not the status of the task or the image we wish to project. The goal is to work; it's not about achieving status or recognition in society. If we can break these mental resistances, we can achieve significant successes. In classical Islamic mysticism, seekers are often encouraged at the outset to engage in humble tasks, such as cleaning. Why? To shatter the self-image, they hold and make them realize they are not as elevated as they think. This is the very point that Ali Asghar Amiri emphasizes. He suggests that alongside education, one should start a business or work in some capacity. But why? Because once you attain a bachelor's or master's degree, a false sense of pride emerges, leading you to shy away from low-level work such as cleaning shops or companies. This false pride causes us to miss many initial opportunities. Thus, it's crucial to jump into work alongside studying and training without fearing lower-level tasks. Understanding that a mindset where no task feels heavy can lead to numerous achievements is essential. Therefore, alongside your studies and training, you should begin your work. If you don't climb the ladder step by step, others will easily surpass you along the way, and you will remain unnoticed. The foundation for high-level management in the future lies in these seemingly trivial actions today.

The Heritage of Our Birthplace

Each of us is born in a place that possesses unique opportunities and qualities. Nowadays, it has become common for some people to deny their birthplace, claiming they have no geographical ties to any specific place. However, the location where we were born, the land we inhabit, and the people around us provide us with invaluable potential that has been offered to us for free. A wise person does not forsake the advantages they already have in pursuit of those they have yet to obtain. If you are born in a place and can benefit from its culture and heritage, why resist it unnecessarily?

Ali Asghar Amiri, a child of the desert and Yazd, embodies this philosophy. He describes his birthplace as a land where people have to work hard to find water and live their lives, which teaches them the importance of managing and valuing their limited resources. Rather than deny where he comes from, this entrepreneur fully embraces the culture of his city to achieve greater success.

What about you? In which city or region were you born? What culture have you inherited? Why do you not view these as valuable legacies? Instead of seeking new things, why not make use of what has been freely given to you? This awareness has driven him since his youth to keep track of every detail, diligently analyzing everything, as we say, with his head in the books. He takes pride in being a son of the desert, a place with scarce resources. The desert has forged him into a resilient man, allowing him to progress in life.

Towards Balance in Work and Life

In life, every gain comes with a cost. It is not possible to gain something without sacrificing something else. As Jack Canfield puts it, you must be willing to pay the price for anything you desire, and everything comes at a cost; no achievement or success is without a price. He points out that an Olympic champion must train five or six hours a day, six days a week, for years to earn a gold medal that may seem trivial to the rest of us. This is the price one must pay.

Similarly, for economic success and achievement in entrepreneurship, you must be willing to pay the necessary price. This might mean spending less time with family, working weekends, and sacrificing rest, all without any guarantee of success. Paying this price requires overcoming inertia and establishing a momentum for movement. Essentially, you must activate a locomotive, which necessitates considerable initial effort. All entrepreneurs understand this.

However, the key point is that you need a strong sense of purpose to endure this process; otherwise, you may find yourself burdened with guilt for neglecting both yourself and your family. Some entrepreneurs proudly recount such sacrifices. There was a famous entrepreneur who missed his father-in-law's funeral because he was busy launching a new factory, justifying that his presence wouldn't change anything and that it was better for him to stay focused on his work. Kim Woo-Choong, in his book "Every Street is Paved with Gold," frequently mentions how he hasn't taken a vacation with his family for years and has even forgotten their birthdays; including his own; and he feels content about it. While someone like Kim Woo-Choong may possess a profound sense of purpose, not everyone can tap into such motivation. What should we do?

The essential question is whether we must choose between these sacrifices. T. Harv Eker notes that a poor mindset thinks in terms of "either/or," while a rich mindset embrace "both/and." For instance, the poor mindset says you must either work hard or enjoy your work, while the rich mindset recognizes that you can both earn a living doing what you love and work diligently at it. This integrative thinking can lead to greater opportunities for discovering possibilities.

The discussion here revolves around whether we should sacrifice our youth, family, and well-being for our work, or if there is an alternative path. Most biographies recount the hard times of diligent work fondly. However, perhaps we can consider a third way: smart and focused work. Once, a writer offered an interesting insight about the Japanese; he claimed they conquered the world with one simple principle: they work diligently throughout all their working hours. He found it incredible that people could maintain such intensity at work. The main issue in our workplaces is the excessive wasted time we experience. Additionally, we are in an era where deep work is scarce, and most people engage in surface-level tasks, undermining job security and professional stability.

With the right approach, you can effectively work throughout your hours with high concentration. If you pursue a field you love, you can excel there; after all, it's said that excellence lies only in what you love. Currently, many developed countries are striving to maximize their employees' vacation time and leisure opportunities, believing that this will enable workers to engage more effectively and yield higher productivity. The goal is productivity, not merely being busy. This brings us to the critical discussion of achieving a balance between work, life, and leisure.

In our religious culture, it is stated that healthy recreational activities play a vital role in enriching human life. Ali Asghar Amiri once mentioned feeling guilty for not living life to its fullest. Despite achieving numerous accomplishments and creating jobs for others, which brings him joy, the underlying point is that we can work a reasonable amount during the day while maximizing our productivity through passion and focus. We can enjoy leisure while also fulfilling our work obligations, deriving satisfaction from both. Sometimes, we need to work intensely to remove obstacles and get the locomotive moving. But once it's in motion, we can restore balance.

Establishing balance doesn't mean working less; it means working intelligently. For instance, by systematizing your business, you may not need to be physically present at your workplace; instead, everything can run according to established and documented procedures. It seems that our entrepreneurs need to be particularly aware of this so that, God forbid, they do not look back in their middle and later years and regret not having truly lived their lives.

Iranian Great Entrepreneurs

A 1000 set of Iranian Great Entrepreneurs

Dr. Reza Yadegari
Mahshid Sanaeefard

The Winners of the Prestigious
Jalal Al-e Ahmad Literary Award

To access Great Entrepreneurs Series

www.ingramcontent.com/pod-product-compliance
Lightning Source LLC
Chambersburg PA
CBHW050225100526
44585CB00017BA/2012